BUSINESS BUILDERS

IN TOYS AND GAMES

Kjeld Kirk and his sister, Hanne, show their LEGO creations to their parents and older sister, Gunhild, in 1962. Kjeld's grandfather, Ole Kirk Christiansen, founded the LEGO company, and his father, Godtfred Kirk, ran the company for many years before Kjeld became head in 1979.

BUSINESS BUILDERS
IN TOYS AND GAMES

Nathan Aaseng

The Oliver Press, Inc.
Minneapolis

The Oliver Press, Inc.
Charlotte Square
5707 West 36th Street
Minneapolis, MN 55416-2510

Library of Congress Cataloging-in-Publication Data
Aaseng, Nathan.
Business builders in toys and games/Nathan Aaseng.
p. cm.
Summary: Provides a history of the toy and game industry and profiles seven people who have
succeeded in that realm.
Includes bibliographical references and index.
Contents: Milton Bradley : The Checkered Game of Life — Albert Spalding : Spalding Sports
Worldwide — Joshua Lionel Cowen : Lionel trains — Ruth Handler : Mattel and the billion
dollar doll — Ole Kirk Christiansen : LEGO Company — Hiroshi Yamauchi : Nintendo —
Gary Gygax : TSR Hobbies, Inc., and Dungeons & Dragons.
ISBN 1-881508-81-1
1. Toy industry—Juvenile literature. 2. Toy making—Juvenile literature. 3. Businesspeople—
Biography—Juvenile literature. [1. Toy industry. 2. Games. 3. Toy making. 4. Businesspeople.]
I. Title.

HD9993.T692 A123 2003
338.7'68872'0922—dc21
[B]   2001059304
                                                   CIP
                                                          AC

ISBN 1-881508-81-1
Printed in the United States of America

09 08 07 06 05 04 03   8 7 6 5 4 3 2 1

CONTENTS

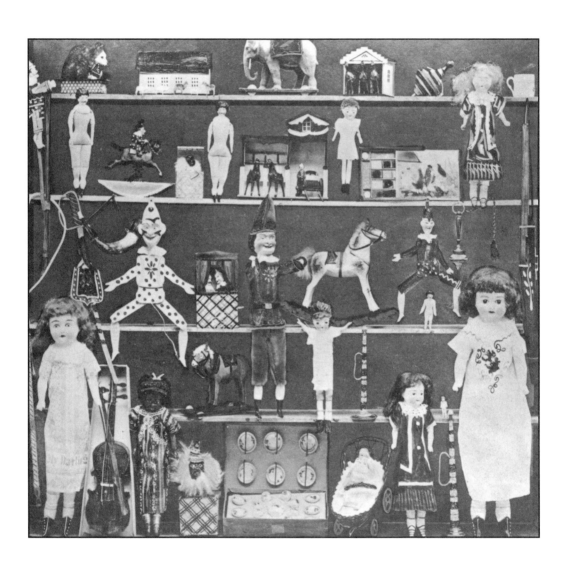

Introduction

THE EVOLUTION OF
TOYS AND GAMES

An otter belly-flops onto a mud chute and slides down into a lake. The family dog quivers with anticipation as her master opens the back door to let her frolic in the yard. A lion cub pounces on his littermate, who joins him in a wrestling match. They are all engaging in play, one of the most curious activities in the animal kingdom.

Humans have never quite known what to make of play. Play does not appear to accomplish any direct survival purpose. Unlike other basic activities such as eating, drinking, and sleeping, it satisfies no immediate physical need. The purpose is simply to provide pleasure—just fun.

Excavations of ancient ruins have determined that basic toys such as balls and dolls have been in use for

Some of the basic toys that have been enjoyed for thousands of years. These were photographed in 1860.

at least 5,000 years, and probably a great deal longer. Author Paul Dickson notes that "small stones, deliberately chipped and rounded, have been unearthed at Stone Age digs on three continents." Archaeologists believe such objects may have been used as marbles.

WASTE OF TIME OR MENTAL THERAPY?

Since play is associated with a lack of accomplishment, society has often looked down on it as a waste of time, despite its long history. For thousands of years, parents have told their children the tale of the ant and the grasshopper. The grasshopper plays all through the summer months while the ant works diligently. When the harsh winter comes, the ant has set aside enough food for its needs, while the grasshopper starves. The lesson is that those who work hard will prosper, while those who play will come to ruin.

On the other hand, there is a general recognition that play provides both mental stimulation and an element of enjoyment, both of which are essential to a person's well-being. The warning of the ant and the grasshopper story is coupled with an opposite proverb, "All work and no play makes Jack a dull boy." The Russian author Leo Tolstoy considered play to be at the heart of existence. "If games were nonsense, what else would there be left to do?" he mused.

These conflicting feelings about play are seen throughout the history of games and toys. Public opinion has swung back and forth between regarding play as a frivolous activity and seeing it as an essential tool for growing up and maintaining mental health.

MILITARY TOYS

Ironically, a number of toys and games that now provide pure entertainment have come directly from one of humanity's grimmest enterprises—war. Some connections between military activity and play were intentional. Anthropologists believe that, in many societies, toys were largely simplified versions of adult tools, and play was designed as a means to learn adult tasks. In this, children were like young lions, whose playful stalking of and pouncing on their littermates prepares them for survival as adults. Thus, in a society in which men hunted and provided protection, boys would play with small replicas of hunting and military weapons.

At other times, however, the relationship between military activity and play was purely accidental. Kites, for example, were used in China around 1200 B.C. as a means of sending coded messages between army camps. Eventually, the military stopped using them, but they were retained by those who enjoyed the thrill of sending a colorful object hundreds of feet into the air.

The game of chess represents another evolution of military activity into play. There is evidence that a game similar to modern chess was played as early as the sixth century. The game probably originated in India, then spread into the Arab countries. The Arabs, in turn, introduced chess to Europeans. By the thirteenth century, chess was played all over

Children playing chess in a New York community center

Western Europe. According to legend, the game was devised as a means of breaking the news to a royal family of the death of a son in battle. The story was told through the actions of game pieces that represented real people. Chess is basically a game of war strategy and, in fact, the first version of the game was called *chaturanga*, or "army."

NOT FOR CHILDREN

Throughout the Middle Ages and until relatively recent times, games and toys were primarily the domain of adults. Children were considered small adults whose irrational natures had to be tamed through work. Leaving them to idle play, according to this belief, allowed them to learn lazy and wicked habits.

Dolls, toy knights, and miniature soldiers that became popular in Europe as early as the fourteenth century were intended mainly for the amusement of adults. This was also true of exotic novelties, such as yo-yos, which date back to 500 B.C. in China, Greece, and Egypt. Because these toys had to be individually handcrafted, they were expensive, and few people could afford the luxury of buying them for their children even if they were so inclined.

Historians trace the beginning of a change in attitude regarding toys and games to the 1690s. At that time, philosopher John Locke proposed that children were not basically evil creatures who had to be tamed and civilized but were more like blank slates, acquiring knowledge by experience and learning. Play, according to Locke, was good for children and could provide them with positive experiences that could shape their character. Nonetheless, the transfer of toys and games into the realm of children was a slow process that took centuries.

In 1689, John Locke (1632-1704) published his most important philosophical work, Essay Concerning Human Understanding.

BIRTH OF THE TOY INDUSTRY

For most of history, the creation of toys and games was the enterprise of either amateurs or a small group of skilled artisans. That began to change in the sixteenth century, when woodsmen in the German city of Nuremberg began carving wooden animals as a way to pass the unproductive winter.

Before long, these Nuremberg carvers gained a reputation for producing finely crafted, imaginative playthings. The better their products, the more people became interested in buying them. The more toys people bought, the more the Nuremberg craftsmen were motivated to increase both the quality and quantity of their products. Around 1760, one of the craftsmen, Andreas Hilpert, branched out from wood into tin, using the metal to make toy soldiers.

Eventually, springs were used to develop wind-up toys that could make a wide range of motions. These products became immensely popular in the nineteenth century. As before, there was no tendency to categorize toys and games as items geared for children; adults were as fascinated as children with the novel examples of mechanical movement.

TOYS AND GAMES IN THE UNITED STATES

While the Nuremberg craftsmen were establishing the basis of a toy industry, people in the United States remained suspicious of the concept of leisure activity. Until the 1860s, toys and games were virtually unknown throughout most of the nation, which was strongly influenced by the demands of wilderness survival and a Puritan work ethic that forbade wasting time at play. The average person lacked not only the motivation to buy these products but also the money and the leisure time to enjoy them.

There were at least three main factors that sparked the growth of the U.S. toy and game industry. The first was a change in attitude. According to historian Gary Cross, as late as the 1890s, "the

Although these toy soldiers (from left to right, Saxon, Roman, and Etruscan) were crafted by Americans in the mid-twentieth century, the artists followed the European tradition for tin soldiers. All two-inch figures are called "tin" regardless of the metal used because the original soldiers made in Germany were cast in tin.

beliefs that children had a right to play and needed specially manufactured objects for this purpose were still rather new." But within a few decades, the public began responding to new, more child-centered educational theories, thus opening a whole new market to the toy industry.

Second, Americans radically changed their gift-giving habits. Prior to the Civil War, giving children toys as birthday presents was practically unheard of. Moreover, Christmas was not recognized as a legal holiday, and those who celebrated the event seldom gave gifts. In the latter half of the nineteenth century, however, individual states began officially sanctioning Christmas as a holiday. As the importance of play in children's lives became accepted, the giving of toys as gifts to celebrate Christmas and birthdays grew into common practice.

The mythical figure of Santa Claus, a kindly and generous old man who brought gifts to children at Christmastime, assumed a permanent place in U.S. culture and created additional demand for toys. Christmas and birthday gift-giving has been the lifeline of the toy and game industry ever since. Even today, the typical toy and game manufacturer counts on the fourth quarter of the year, the Christmas season, for up to 70 percent of its sales. Birthday gift sales account for a significant portion of the remaining 30 percent.

A third factor spurred on the toy and game industry: industrialization. When New England manufacturers such as Milton Bradley established themselves in business with games and wind-up toys

A classic Christmas scene: pajama-clad children admire their new toy train traveling around the Christmas tree.

following the Civil War, many of these products were so expensive that the average person could not afford to buy them. By 1920, however, U.S. manufacturing had increased to nearly 14 times its level in 1860. This had a remarkable effect on toy and game products. New methods of mass production, the use of efficient machines instead of human labor, and the development of newer, cheaper materials all helped make toys and games affordable to the common person for the first time in history.

The rapidly growing U.S. industry eventually shifted the center of influence in the toy and game industry from Germany to the U.S. In 1900, Germany ranked as the undisputed leader in the business. It exported 75 percent of its products, with one-fourth going to the United States. American toys were generally considered to be of inferior quality. But U.S. toy manufacturers improved their products with novel items such as Tinker Toys, Lincoln Logs, and Erector sets, all of which appeared between 1909 and 1914. These toys steadily cut into the German market. Then, during World War I, German manufacturers could not export toys to the countries they were fighting. This, along with lingering bitterness at the war's end, drastically reduced Germany's toy and game sales and allowed the U.S. to vault past it in the industry. By 1939, 95 percent of the toys sold in the United States were manufactured within the country, compared to 50 percent in 1905.

THE MODERN TOY INDUSTRY

The first half of the twentieth century served as a transition period between the era of toyless childhoods and today's children, who are targeted by toy and game manufacturers. During this transition time, toys and games served as a shared experience between generations. Family members of all ages could play one of Milton Bradley's many games. Parents as well as children were fascinated by the challenge of A. C. Gilbert's Erector sets and captivated by Lionel's realistic miniature train sets. Prominent toy and game companies such as Parker Brothers, Fisher-Price, Gilbert, Playskool, Hasbro, and Marx marketed primarily to parents, who delighted in giving their children dolls and games and train sets, which they themselves had never been able to enjoy as youngsters.

That began to change in the 1950s with the popularity of television. Toy and game manufacturers found that they could be more effective in aiming their sales pitches at the group that now generated the most demand for their products: children. The result of this switch, according to author Gary Cross, was that "since the late 1960s many old toy companies, venerated for manufacturing toys passed from one generation to the next, have disappeared," and "in their place have come a new breed of companies that specialize in novelty and appeal directly to the imaginations of children."

Mass marketing took over the toy and game business. Smaller manufacturing companies found themselves unable to compete with the large companies. On the retail sales end of the business, the establishment of giant toy stores such as Toys R Us, Inc., which opened in 1957, drove small shopowners out of business. Toy companies soon discovered that although they could create an overnight sensation with a fad such as Hula Hoops or Silly Putty, they needed huge expenditures of advertising cash to keep afloat between bursts of success. By 1980, television advertising was not only driving the toy and game

Toys R Us, Inc., founder Charles Lazarus sold baby furniture, then added the toys his customers often requested. He opened his first toy supermarket in 1957. His stores were successful, and he sold them to another company, Interstate. When Interstate later filed for bankruptcy, Lazarus joined the company and made the stores profitable once again. Toys R Us, Inc., became a public company in 1978. As of 2002, the toy giant had 1,600 stores worldwide generating $11 billion in business.

Hula Hoop champion Lori Lynn Lomeli demonstrates her skill with this toy. She broke her own world record in 2001, spinning 83 hoops simultaneously. Lomeli's previous record, set in 1999, was 82.

business, it was also consuming it. In the fall of 1985, all top 10 best-selling toys in the U.S. were tied into cartoon television shows.

Federal regulations against developing television shows that sell products to children have since diminished the influence of this type of program. The need for large cash reserves to fund advertising, however, is as strong as ever. Advertising for toys and games now approaches $1 billion annually.

Serving Dish or Toy?

One of the best examples of the unpredictable nature of the toy business is the story of the Frisbee. Although widely seen as a relatively recent invention, the Frisbee traces its origins back more than a century. Like many toys, its original purpose had nothing to do with play.

It all started in 1871 when William Russell Frisbie bought a bakery in Bridgeport, Connecticut. Frisbie's sister baked pies while he took care of sales and delivery. Before long, the Frisbies were doing a brisk business that included sales to the nearby city of New Haven, home of Yale University. The pies were baked and delivered on metal plates that bore the name of the Frisbie Pie Company. Sometime after the turn of the century, Yale students discovered that these pie plates flew nicely when thrown and began to play catch with them. Players would shout "Frisbie!" to warn an unsuspecting bystander of an errant pie plate toss.

Playing with "Frisbies" became a local tradition that spread to other parts of the country when Yale students returned to their hometowns. But no one thought of manufacturing them as a toy until the 1940s. At that time, Walter Frederick Morrison, a U.S. soldier, wondered if there were some way to capitalize on the flurry of stories sweeping the country about sightings of unidentified flying objects. Many of the reports compared the shape of the UFOs to saucers.

Morrison, although he knew nothing about the Frisbie, came up with the idea of selling a sort of flying saucer toy.

He used a pie plate, but tried to improve its flight by welding a steel rim inside it. He was dissatisfied with the result. A flash of inspiration prompted him to try plastic. According to Morrison, "It worked fine as long as the sun was up, but then the thing got brittle, and if you didn't catch it, it would break into a million pieces. We worked that out. We offered to replace any broken one with a new one, *if* they brought back every piece!"

Morrison worked on improving his flying saucer toy. He used a more flexible kind of plastic, and the new saucers were durable and flew well. Eventually, Morrison's flying saucers attracted the attention of two young men newly graduated from the University of Southern California. These men, Rich Knerr and A. K. Melin, were already making slingshots, and they hooked up with Morrison to start producing and marketing his flying platters in 1957. They called the new line "Wham-O" flying saucers, but the name never caught on. The Wham-O Company decided to revert to the old name of the pie plate that students had known for decades. It registered its redesigned version under the name "Frisbee." (Knerr did not know how to spell the original "Frisbie," so he spelled it "Frisbee.")

Although between 3,000 and 6,000 new toys are introduced to the market each year, few become established as profitable products. The expense and uncertainties of competing in the toy and game industry have created a trend toward mergers and acquisitions as the smaller, struggling companies are forced to sell out to the larger companies in order to survive. The flurry of toy and game company

Beaches offer an ideal setting for tossing a Frisbee. The wind can make the saucer's flight unpredictable, there is plenty of room to run, and there is always the possibility of getting wet.

merger: an agreement that combines two or more corporations into one

transactions began in the late 1960s with Milton Bradley buying Playskool, Quaker Oats taking over Fisher-Price, and General Mills assuming control of Parker Brothers. It has accelerated to the point that, in the twenty-first century, many of the best-known names in the industry, including Playskool, Parker Brothers, Ideal, Coleco, and Tonka Toys, have all been absorbed by a single corporation—Hasbro.

THE TOY GIANT

Hasbro has, in fact, acquired two of the toy companies featured in this book: Milton Bradley and TSR Hobbies, Inc. The Hassenfeld brothers, who founded Hasbro, were immigrants from Poland. Henry and Helal Hassenfeld settled in Providence, Rhode Island, where they sold fabric remnants beginning in 1923. The Hassenfelds ran a close-knit family business—all eight of their original employees were relatives.

Eventually the Hassenfelds began using the fabric to make pencil boxes and pouches filled with school supplies. When their pencil supplier raised prices in 1935, the Hassenfelds decided they could do better making their own pencils. They started the Empire Pencil Company, which grew into the largest pencil manufacturer in the U.S. During the 1940s, Henry's son Merrill—who had by that time become company president—suggested that they expand into making toys to fill the downtime when school supplies were not selling. The company, which became known as Hasbro (short for Hassenfeld Brothers) began marketing paint sets and crayons.

Hasbro grew steadily but unremarkably. It first achieved national recognition in 1951 with the introduction of the popular toy Mr. Potato Head. In 1964, Hasbro developed the forerunner of the action toy, an 11½-inch World War II soldier named G. I. Joe, fully equipped with combat gear. In two years, Hasbro sold more than 8 million G. I. Joe figures.

A third generation of Hassenfelds, Stephen and Alan, took over the company in the mid-1970s. Stephen Hassenfeld's goal: "Five, ten, fifteen years from now, I'd like to be the General Motors of the toy business." General Motors was then the largest corporation in the world.

The new bosses ran into some early financial trouble, which thwarted their plans for a while. But in the 1980s, Hasbro made its move. It bought out successful toys such as the My Little Pony figures and inventive action toys called Transformers. Then it went on a buying spree that was to last two decades. In 1984, the company purchased game manufacturer Milton Bradley, which also held the rights to Playskool Toys and Lincoln Logs. In quick succession Hasbro added Parker Brothers, as well as Coleco's Cabbage Patch dolls, the hit board game Scrabble, and Tonka Toys. These acquisitions enabled Hasbro to overtake Mattel (maker of the Barbie doll) as the world's largest toy and game manufacturer by the early 1990s, fulfilling Stephen Hassenfeld's wish—for a few years. By 2001, Mattel was back in the lead.

In 1994, Hasbro produced this 30th anniversary replica of its original 11½-inch G.I. Joe. The smaller, 3-inch soldiers, introduced later, remain popular with children as well as collectors.

SURPRISED BY SUCCESS

The people who built the toy and game industry into a multibillion-dollar business have shown the same mixed feelings as the rest of society about the value of toys and games. Almost without exception, they started their careers focused on other areas of work, with no intention of dealing in toys. The lives of the pioneers in the toy and game industry are filled with as many surprises and unexpected turns as any board game ruled by the roll of the dice.

Milton Bradley was trying to establish himself in the photographic print business when a bad break pushed him into game manufacturing. Joshua Lionel Cowen, an electronics whiz, was not thinking of toys when he designed his first electric train.

Albert Spalding and Gary Gygax both chose careers in the insurance business and took up games only after those careers fizzled. Hiroshi Yamauchi was studying law when he took over the family business, Nintendo, and turned it into a leading maker of electronic games. Ruth Handler and her husband started Mattel to manufacture plastic picture frames. Ole Kirk Christiansen's LEGO Company arose out of a struggling carpentry shop.

Given the nature of play, these stories of accidental success are a fitting tribute to the business builders in toys and games. For as any child can attest, fun is often spontaneous, and the greatest inspirations for toys and games have a way of catching people by surprise.

Ole Kirk Christiansen working in his shop

Betty James and Slinky

Betty James is among those toy manufacturers who were surprised by success. And the continued popularity of the simple Slinky—it's been springing around almost 60 years now—has surprised many in the toy industry.

Richard James invented the Slinky in 1945. A naval engineer, James was conducting an experiment with springs when one of them fell to the floor and began to "walk." He took it home to show his wife, Betty. She thought it would make a great toy and named it Slinky.

A year later, Slinky debuted at Gimbel's department store in Philadelphia. Doubts about the toy's appeal disappeared as all 400 Slinkys sold in just 90 minutes.

But the story doesn't stop there. In 1960, Richard joined a cult and moved to Bolivia. He left Betty their business, James Industries, and six children aged 2 to 18. She sold the Philadelphia factory, moved her operation to Hollidaysburg, Pennsylvania, near her hometown of Altoona, and went back to work.

Betty James is proud that her toy is still affordable, fun, and selling well. Here she stands in front of a poster of the stamp issued by the U.S. Postal Service honoring Slinky.

In 1995, Slinky celebrated its 50th anniversary. That year the company added a star to its product line, a redesigned Slinky dog that had charmed audiences in Disney's animated movie *Toy Story*. James Industries struggled to keep the cute canines on toy-store shelves.

Three years later, James sold her company to Poof Products, Inc., a toymaker in Plymouth, Michigan. Slinkys are still manufactured in Hollidaysburg, and Betty's son, Tom James, stayed on to manage the operation. Although she is no longer involved in day-to-day business concerns, Betty James continues to promote Slinky.

She also likes to tell the story of the day she was a "heroine." Her two youngest children were home sick and bored, so she brought them Slinkys. They had never played with the toy before. James had been so busy, "it never even occurred to me to bring them home," she said. But that day, like millions of other parents have done, she showed her delighted children how Slinky walks down the stairs.

1

MILTON BRADLEY

THE UNPREDICTABLE GAME OF LIFE

"A picture is worth a thousand words" is an old cliché. Milton Bradley found out, however, that sometimes a few dozen words can be worth many thousands of pictures. A short, whimsical letter, penned by an 11-year-old girl to the future president of the United States, drove Bradley out of the portrait business and into a new career.

As it turned out, what seemed an incredible stroke of bad luck launched him on the path to fame and fortune. In a case of life imitating art, the creator of a popular board game learned that even the best-planned career can change direction with one spin of the wheel.

Milton Bradley (1836-1911) planned to become a printer, but instead used his presses to manufacture board games, some of which are still played today.

Milton Bradley was born in Vienna, Maine, on November 8, 1836. His father was a minister and taught Milton the importance of good morals from an early age. Lewis Bradley hammered home the idea that people reap what they sow. Those who practice good deeds, said Lewis, will be rewarded, while those who do wrong will get their just punishment.

At some point in his young life, Milton became interested in playing board games, an activity that religious leaders of his era discouraged as promoting idleness. Games whose purpose was to promote good morals or religious instruction were exceptions to this rule, though, such as Lottery of the Pious, first printed by Christopher Sower in 1744, and Ann Abbott's Mansion of Happiness, invented in 1843.

As much as he enjoyed games, Bradley knew better than to take them too seriously, even if they did have a morality theme. He focused his energy on finding a career. After graduating from high school, he tried working as a draftsman and selling stationery in his off hours.

Unsatisfied, he moved in with his parents, who had relocated to Cambridge, Massachusetts, and went back to school, enrolling in a two-year course of study at the Lawrence Scientific School. Bradley had come within a few months of completing the course when his parents decided to move to Springfield, Massachusetts. Milton could not afford to pay for both board and tuition, so he gave up his schooling and moved to Springfield with them.

A NEW INTEREST

In 1860, Bradley devised his own version of a morality game, borrowing some elements of existing games, and called it The Checkered Game of Life. His game moved players along a checkerboard on a path from Infancy to Happy Old Age. Some squares were marked with positive values and others were marked with negative attributes and misfortune. Landing on desirable squares moved a person up, while landing on vices set a player back. Bradley's game clearly spelled out the connections between moral virtues and vices and the consequences they produced. For example, landing on the Bravery square allowed a player to move up to Honor, while landing on the Gambling square sent the player back to Ruin. Bradley took

Players who landed on "virtuous" spaces were the winners in Bradley's The Checkered Game of Life.

copies of the game to New York to sell to small store-owners, and it turned out to be so popular that he came back without a single leftover copy.

When Bradley became interested in the process of lithography later that year, he set his game aside and concentrated on his new interest. Lithography is a form of printing that can reproduce pictures, even photographs, with the use of a carefully prepared master printing plate. Milton Bradley traveled to Providence, Rhode Island, to get training in lithographic techniques. When he returned to Springfield, he bought a printing press and went into business.

A PORTRAIT OF LINCOLN

The decision as to what to print on his presses could make or break his new business, and Bradley came up with a sure-fire winner. A local reporter returned to Springfield with a photograph of Abraham Lincoln from the Republican Party convention in Chicago at which Lincoln was nominated for president. Bradley acquired rights to the photograph and printed off thousands of copies, which he expected to sell for a handsome profit.

Bradley's expectations were based on sound business sense. According to historian Gabor S. Boritt, "In an age without cinema or television, when few periodicals were illustrated and newspapers were still unable to reproduce photographs in their papers, pictures were precious. . . . Americans sought images of their political heroes as the youth of today seek posters of rock stars."

The portrait of Abraham Lincoln that Bradley reproduced during the 1860 presidential election

Some of the established print companies, such as Currier & Ives, produced lithographed portraits of a wide variety of candidates to attract customers of all political beliefs. Bradley, though, concentrated his resources on Lincoln. As the presidential candidate most strongly opposed to slavery, Lincoln was especially popular in Massachusetts, one of the hotbeds of the abolitionist movement. Furthermore, Lincoln had risen to national prominence almost overnight. As a result, there were few portraits of him available. Many lithographers were scrambling to find portraits of Lincoln to meet the large demand, and Bradley was fortunate to have obtained one.

GRACE BEDELL'S LETTER

What Bradley and other lithographers did not know was that, shortly before the election, 11-year-old Grace Bedell from Westfield, New York, had written her favorite presidential candidate to give him some advice. Bedell suggested Lincoln grow a beard, because, as she argued, "you would look a great deal better for your face is so thin. All the ladies like whiskers and they would tease their husbands to vote for you."

While the advice was highly doubtful as a campaign strategy, Lincoln found it intriguing. Having endured a great deal of abuse from political opponents who derided him as ugly, he decided to give the new look a try. By the time Lincoln arrived in Washington for the inauguration, the United States had its first bearded president.

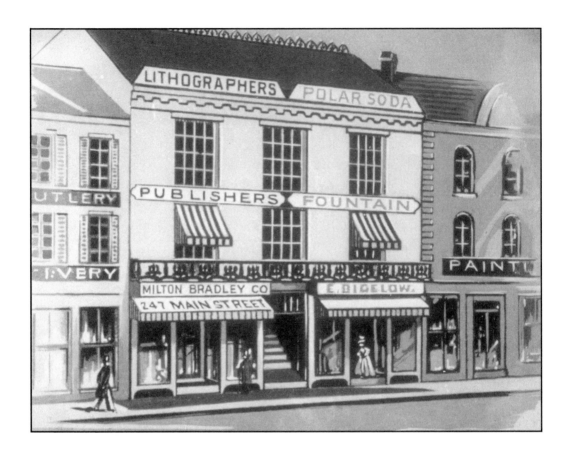

Milton Bradley's lithography shop in Springfield, Massachusetts

Bradley and the other portrait sellers were caught off guard by the change and found themselves stuck with out-of-date pictures. Bradley was stunned by his bad luck. He saw no choice but to destroy his obsolete lithographic plates and prints.

NEW CAREER

At around the same time, Milton Bradley began receiving orders for The Checkered Game of Life. Because he had nothing else to print with his idle presses, he decided to focus on producing the game.

There was little competition in the United States game manufacturing business at the time. The W. & S. B. Ives company had held the field largely to itself since about 1843. Another game manufacturer, John McLoughlin, had just recently started a business to produce beautiful handcrafted games. Beyond that, Bradley saw a void in the game industry just waiting to be filled. He recognized that new lithographic techniques would make it possible, for the first time, to mass-produce colorful boxed games. By pasting lithographed sheets of paper onto cardboard, Bradley cranked out thousands of copies of his game. He traveled around New England and New York selling his product.

As a game that preached moral values, The Checkered Game of Life found a receptive audience in the northern states, especially in New England. There a large core of vocal activists were rallying the public to fight a great moral crusade to end slavery. Bradley's The Checkered Game of Life sold over 40,000 copies in 1861, which made it the most popular game in the nation. Also important to his success, Bradley hit upon the idea of putting together pocket-sized game kits for Union soldiers (who had begun fighting the Civil War earlier that year) to help break the monotony of their long weeks of training.

MILTON BRADLEY: EDUCATOR

The success of The Checkered Game of Life persuaded Bradley to reorganize his company for the mass production and sale of games and toys. He planned to make use of lithography to give his toys a bright, attractive appearance, and he continued to focus his efforts on products with a moral or instructional purpose. Bradley also manufactured optical instruments and school supplies, and he soon became an advocate of the movement to offer kindergarten in U.S. schools.

Bradley's educational focus led him to market a new product called the Historiscope as a method of studying history. Introduced in 1868, the Historiscope was basically a box with a roller on either side. A long strip of paper, on which a series of illustrations of important events in U.S. history was printed, could be wound between the rollers. One side of the box was cut away so that a person could view the illustrations as they wound through the opening.

ASTUTE BUSINESSMAN

Bradley proved to be an astute businessman as well as a salesman. In the 1860s, he obtained a U.S. patent on the Zoetrope, a device that had been invented in Europe in 1852. The Zoetrope was based on the same principle used in the Historiscope. It consisted of a metal drum into which slits were cut at regular intervals. Inside the drum were illustrated panels on paper strips. Each panel showed people or objects in a scene at various stages of movement. The drum was rotated rapidly on its base, and the panels flashed by in quick succession, giving the appearance of an animated scene. (The Zoetrope established some of the basic principles that would lead to the development of motion pictures.) Rather

Milton Bradley's two daughters were among the first kindergarten students in Springfield. Bradley, his wife, and his father were the first kindergarten teachers. Bradley developed blocks and other toys to teach basic skills, which he called Kindergarten Gifts. He added these gifts to his company's products and as kindergartens became accepted into public school systems, orders poured in.

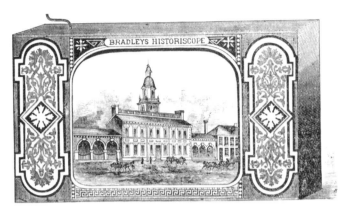

THE POPULAR ZOETROPE.

The Historiscope (top) and the Zoetrope were popular devices in the 1860s.

than attempt to manufacture this complicated device himself, Bradley leased the rights to other companies and earned himself a tidy profit.

lease: a contract granting the use of property for a specified time in exchange for payment

EXPANDING COMPANY

Bradley relentlessly expanded his line of products from year to year. In the late 1860s, he developed and marketed the first croquet set made in the United States. In 1870, he expanded into a new line of educational products that would prove to be one of his most popular and enduring additions: jigsaw puzzles. Many of Bradley's early puzzles were basically cut-up maps designed to help children learn geography. But he expanded the subject matter to include puzzles such as his Smashed Up Locomotive: A Mechanical Puzzle for Boys.

Again, Bradley took advantage of advances in technology to move to the forefront of the industry. Jigsaw puzzles had previously been individually sawed out of wood. A new technique allowed him to use a cutting die that could cut through sheet after sheet of cardboard, producing puzzles more easily and cheaply. At the same time, Bradley continued to manufacture an ever-growing series of board games. Bamboozle, introduced in 1876, was especially noteworthy because it contained the first large folding game board. Today's typical commercial game board is nearly identical to the 18-by-18-inch Bamboozle board.

THE GAME OF BAMBOOZLE.

The game Bamboozle (top) featured the first folding game board. Bradley's Smashed Up Locomotive (right) was one of his customers' favorite jigsaw puzzles.

Bradley's success grew, even though he did not win good reviews for artwork or sturdiness of construction. Bradley's games did not have the high quality of McLoughlin games, but Bradley was prolific; he was able to mass-produce his games. By 1876, Bradley was one of the nation's leading game manufacturers. That same year, the Milton Bradley Company was honored with a Medal of Excellence at the nation's Centennial Exposition, which was "the first award ever made for ethical teaching of children through play."

LATER YEARS

Over the next two decades, Bradley continued to market his games to children and families with such offerings as Chuba (a version of the ancient African game Mancala) and The Yale-Harvard Game (a football game). In the 1880s, a new rival, George Parker, arose to challenge Milton Bradley's supremacy in the game industry. Parker and his brothers broke ground in creating strategy games for adults and introducing card games such as Pit and Rook in the 1900s. But there was enough overlap in Bradley's and Parker's products to create a fierce competition. Bradley moved aggressively to keep his position as the game industry leader by opening offices nationwide. By 1903, he had offices in New York, Atlanta, San Francisco, Philadelphia, and Boston, as well as Springfield.

Smaller game manufacturers could not compete with the growing might of the emerging giants. One by one, they closed up shop. By the time of his

Jigsaw puzzles, which had been sold in Europe for more than a century, were so named because a jigsaw was required to perform the intricate cutting of the wood into the oddly shaped pieces.

death in 1911, Milton Bradley had clearly established his company as one of the best-known brand names in the nation.

LEGACY

The company that Milton Bradley founded continued to prosper long after his death by following his basic formula of concentrating on children and families. The Milton Bradley Company enjoyed almost continual growth, except when World War II forced it to reduce its line of products from 410 items to 150. Even during that crisis, the company introduced one of its most popular games ever, Chutes and Ladders (1943). Developed from an ancient game from India called Snakes and Ladders, it followed the same pattern of rewards and consequences that Milton Bradley had used in The Checkered Game of Life more than 80 years earlier. Milton Bradley's other best-selling games included Candy Land (1949) and Twister (1966). In 1960, the company produced a 100th anniversary revival of the Game of Life that was modernized and more concerned with acquiring wealth than eternal bliss.

In a more general sense, Milton Bradley helped shape the United States game industry for nearly a century. He was the first to use mass production techniques, which made board games affordable to the average person. His portable Civil War game kits introduced the concept of the travel game, which blossomed many decades later in the age of automobile transportation. In the 1870s, he established the basic size and shape of the game board that has

remained the standard. In 1950, the Milton Bradley Company marketed The Hopalong Cassidy Game, the first game based on a television series, setting a trend that would sweep the culture over the next several decades.

In 1984, after 124 years as a family-owned company, the Milton Bradley company was sold to toy industry giant Hasbro. But its main facilities in East Longmeadow, Massachusetts, continue to employ about 1,500 people, and its name still graces the covers of the familiar games and puzzles that it has introduced to the world during its long existence.

For more than 50 years, young Candy Land players have been skipping across the Gumdrop Pass or getting lost in Lollipop Woods.

Bradley's Rival: Monopoly from Parker

George Parker of Salem, Massachusetts, was a game fanatic. He invented his first game, called Banking, in 1883, when he was 16. He persuaded his high-school principal to allow him a three-week leave of absence so he could produce and sell 500 copies of the game in time for Christmas.

Although he nearly sold out his stock, his parents were not impressed. They preferred that he stop playing games and settle down to a serious career. Although he kept his company going on the side, Parker took up a career as a journalist. But while working for the *Boston Commercial Bulletin* in 1886, he developed a severe respiratory illness. Doctors advised him to seek a less strenuous profession, which gave Parker a good excuse to go into the game business full-time.

In 1888, he and his brother Charles joined forces to form Parker Brothers. Another brother, Edward, joined them in 1898, by which time the company had already become one of the leading game manufacturers in the United States.

Inventing games is an inexact science. The most popular board game of all time, Monopoly, was initially rejected by Parker Brothers. After play-testing the game, executives said it took too long to play, contained 52 playing errors, and would never sell.

Monopoly was invented by Elizabeth Magie, a Quaker from Virginia, as a way of illustrating her argument that a person's tax should be based on the amount of land he or she owned. The Landlord's Game, which she patented in 1904, set out the basic layout of the board, including 40 spaces, 4 railroad squares, 2 utilities, 22 rental properties, and a space each for jail, go to jail, luxury tax, and parking.

The Landlord's Game became popular not only with Magie's friends but also among college students in the eastern United States. The game took on a life of its own among its enthusiasts, who phased out Magie's complicated tax implications and left it as a race for financial domination that became known as Monopoly.

Magie incorporated some of these changes into her game, allowing players to improve their properties and earn higher rents if they gained a monopoly. But when she attempted to interest Parker Brothers in her product, they declined, saying the game was too political.

Meanwhile, thousands of people continued to play homemade versions of Monopoly. In Atlantic City, a group of friends named the streets on their homemade game boards after local streets. It was this Atlantic City version that a friend brought to the home of Charles Darrow in 1933. Darrow had lost his job as a sales representative for a heating equipment firm in 1930 and, because of the nation's economic depression, had been unable to find work since.

He enjoyed the game so much that he made a few revisions, copyrighted the Atlantic City board, and began to make copies of it for his friends. Within a few months, Darrow received so many requests for the game that he either had to start his own business or find an established company to help him. He approached Parker Brothers, but they rejected him, leading Darrow to borrow money to go into business for himself. Darrow's big break came when an executive at Wanamaker's department store in Philadelphia ordered 5,000 copies—which quickly sold out.

Word of the success of Monopoly reached the people at Parker Brothers, who changed their minds and bought the rights to the game, including Magie's patents, in 1935. The hugely popular Monopoly helped turn Parker Brothers' fortunes around. It became the best-selling board game of all time and is now printed in 26 languages and sold around the world.

2

ALBERT SPALDING

A. G. SPALDING & BROTHERS: EQUIPPED TO PLAY

Given the choice between working in the business office of a grocery store or signing on as the star pitcher for a professional baseball team, most people would choose the baseball career without a moment's thought. Albert G. Spalding had that choice, yet even after thinking long and hard, he turned down several tempting offers from the nation's best baseball teams—in favor of going into the grocery business! Even when he lost his job with the grocery, Spalding continued to shun the life of a celebrity sports hero.

Only after repeated failures as a bookkeeper did he finally give in to the lure of the baseball diamond. But even then he refused to let go of his preoccupation with business. All the while he was pitching

Albert Spalding (1850-1915) pitched baseballs: first as a star professional player and then as a businessman for his sporting-goods store. The company he founded continues to make balls and other equipment needed to play a variety of sports.

his team to championships, this Hall-of-Fame athlete was hard at work laying the foundation for a business that would long outlast his baseball fame.

BASEBALL TALENT

Albert Goodwill Spalding was born on September 2, 1850, in the small town of Byron, Illinois, about 90 miles northwest of Chicago. In 1863, the family moved to nearby Rockford. While attending school there, Spalding learned to play a relatively new game that was spreading throughout the country—baseball. The strapping, six-foot, one-inch youth gained a reputation for throwing a baseball harder than anyone.

After finishing classes at a commercial college in Rockford with a view toward becoming a businessman, Spalding started his career as a grocery clerk, earning five dollars a week. In the meantime, the Forest City Club of Rockford, the team for which he played baseball, grew so successful that it was invited to travel to Washington, D.C., in 1867, for a series of exhibition games. Spalding's overpowering performance as the team's pitcher led his Forest City Club to victory over some of the top teams in the nation. Immediately, professional baseball owners in the East lined up to recruit him for their teams. Spalding returned home to Rockford with a pocket full of offers from teams in Washington, Cleveland, and New York, including a contract that would pay him $2,500 a year to play.

contract: a legally binding, written agreement between two or more people

Although $2,500 a year was nearly 10 times Albert Spalding's salary as a clerk, his family was not impressed. Character was far more important than money to Albert's widowed mother, Harriet, who did not like the idea of her son getting a big head as a famous ballplayer. In addition, most Americans opposed the idea of athletes getting paid to play sports. Sports were considered a wholesome activity only when people played for the sheer fun of it. In the 1860s, accusations that people were taking money for playing sports created minor scandals in many parts of the country.

Harriet persuaded her son to forsake the vanity of a sports career and instead turn to the solid, respectable world of business. Albert Spalding rejected the baseball contracts and accepted a position in the business office of a wholesale grocery store in Chicago. Instead of being rewarded for making what he thought was the honorable choice, however, Spalding was pummeled by an incredible series of disasters. The grocery store went out of business before Spalding had been there a year. Spalding then found work at an insurance company but had barely settled into the job before that company also went bankrupt.

bankrupt: having been legally determined unable to pay back one's debts

Shell-shocked by his bad luck in the big city, he returned to Rockford, where he took a job as a bookkeeper with a newspaper. That company lasted no longer than the others, and Spalding moved on to a position as bookkeeper in an insurance agency. Sure enough, that company closed its doors for good a few months later. In the five years after he rejected the baseball offer, Spalding worked for seven different companies, all of which folded shortly after he arrived. Although none of the failures was his fault, Spalding could not help doubting his business sense and feeling as though he were under the spell of a bizarre curse.

EARLY AMERICAN BASEBALL STAR

These traumatic experiences persuaded him that he could hardly do worse with his life by playing baseball. By 1871, the practice of paying professionals to play baseball had become more accepted. The desperate Spalding got up the courage to go against his mother's wishes, and he signed with the Boston Red Stockings. On May 5, 1871, he began a brief but remarkably successful professional career.

The underhanded pitching delivery that baseball required in Spalding's time did not put nearly the strain on the arm that today's overhand style does, and so teams depended on their top pitcher to pitch virtually every game. Spalding did so with Boston and pitched the team to the championship of the National Association of Professional Base Ball Players in his first season. With Spalding dominating opposing hitters, the Red Stockings won the championship for the next four seasons.

Boston was so overpowering that fans of some of the opposing teams lost interest in the game, and overall attendance suffered. During those five seasons, Spalding became the first professional pitcher

In Spalding's time, baseball rules were far different from what they are today. The primary object was for batters to hit the ball. Pitchers had to throw the ball underhanded to a location specified by the batter. Batters did not have to swing at pitches that missed the location. Every third pitch that fell outside this area was called a ball; the other misses were simply ignored. Under these rules, strikeouts and walks were extremely rare. Even some of the best pitchers did little more than serve up good pitches for the batters to hit. Spalding's unique talent was the ability to throw the ball so hard that even when he threw it exactly where the batters requested, they had a tough time making solid contact.

Albert G. Spalding in his Boston baseball uniform. The Boston Red Stockings started paying its players in 1869, before it was an acceptable practice.

to win 200 games. By 1875, he was virtually unbeatable, winning 24 games in a row. He was credited with 207 of Boston's 227 victories during his stint with the team, and he showed his all-around athletic ability by compiling a .320 average as a batter.

MOVING BACK INTO BUSINESS

Yet while becoming one of the nation's first baseball heroes, Spalding never lost sight of his original goal to succeed in business. At the time, there were no strict standards for the manufacturing of baseballs, so the idea occurred to him that making a superior quality baseball could be profitable, especially if the popularity of the sport continued to grow. Spalding constantly experimented with different versions of baseballs during his career. By 1876, he had developed what he believed was the finest baseball ever made. Spalding's baseball started with a small center of cork wrapped in two layers of soft rubber for a total weight of $7/8$ of an ounce. The ball then went through four series of windings. The first series used 121 yards of rough gray wool, then 45 yards of fine white wool. This was followed by 53 yards of fine gray wool and 150 yards of fine white cotton. The horsehide cover was then handstitched on with 108 stitches of waxed twine.

When William Hulbert, one of the owners of the Chicago White Stockings, organized the loose federation of professional teams into a more structured National League, Albert Spalding saw his chance. He accepted Hulbert's offer to come back to the Midwest and play for the White Stockings. Then, in February 1876, he helped Hulbert establish the new league. Counting on the new league to boost the popularity of baseball, Spalding and his brother, J. Walter Spalding, opened a baseball goods store in Chicago the next month. A huge sign painted over the door announced, "Spalding has gone into the baseball business."

In 1876, the first year of the National League, Spalding worked hard to make the White Stockings and the National League a success. He served as the

Spalding tested his baseballs to exacting quality control standards. Each ball had to be between 5 and 5.25 ounces in weight, had to distort less than 0.3 inches when compressed between two heavy weights, and had to be able to withstand being pounded with a 65-pound weight 200 times without losing its roundness.

White Stockings' manager and star pitcher. Spalding pitched 61 of the team's 66 games and worked an astounding 528 innings. He posted a 47-12 record, and, despite the rules that favored the hitters, he limited opposing teams to fewer than two runs per game. Under Spalding's leadership, the White Stockings easily won the pennant, and a solid foundation was laid for the new league.

Demand for the Spalding baseball grew quickly. Spalding paid close attention to quality control so that his customers could count on every one of his baseballs to be exactly the same weight and size, have the same bounce, and be durable. In 1877, National League owners repaid Spalding for his contributions to the league by declaring his product to be the league's official baseball.

That same year, Spalding cut back drastically on his playing time right at the height of his career. He stopped pitching and limited himself to third base. After playing only one game in 1878, he quit the sport altogether at the age of 28. No one is sure why. Perhaps he simply preferred the challenge of running his company or he may have remained uncomfortable with his mother's disapproval of his career.

SELLING THE GAME OF BASEBALL

Demand for the Spalding baseball grew so rapidly that Spalding built a new company headquarters, located in Chicopee, Massachusetts. Not satisfied with the profits from the baseballs, Spalding began manufacturing and selling other baseball equipment,

Chicago White Stockings pitcher John Tener in 1888 or 1889. He played for the team under Spalding's ownership and is, no doubt, holding a Spalding baseball.

such as gloves and catcher's masks. Business continued to grow, which encouraged Spalding to open a new store in New York City in 1885.

During the 1880s, rumors of gambling scandals in which baseball players had fixed games shook the confidence of the public. Increasing incidents of drunkenness and brawling at baseball games, even among the players, further eroded interest among respectable citizens. Spalding believed that the newly formed American Association was the main cause of these problems. The American Association teams played on Sundays, allowed alcohol to be sold at games, and charged less admission than the National League did for its games. Looking to protect both the sport he loved and his fledgling business, Spalding became president and owner of the White Stockings and initiated negotiations with the American Association to persuade its teams to clean up their games. In 1883, the rival leagues signed the National Agreement, which gave each league control over its own territory and established some basic rules.

Spalding's next effort on behalf of baseball was a highly publicized world tour from October 1888 to April 1889. He took his Chicago team and an All-American team on a six-month journey around the world to stimulate international interest in baseball. Spalding also promoted major-league baseball by editing an annual book of statistics and other information, which he called *Spalding's Official Baseball Guide.*

The cover of the 1913 edition of Spalding's Official Baseball Guide

The Origins of Baseball

So zealous was Spalding in promoting baseball that he bears a large responsibility for creating a myth about the origins of the game. He took it upon himself to settle debates about whether baseball was an American game or a version of an English game called rounders by recruiting a seven-person commission to study the issue. In 1907, his commission reported that the sport originated in Cooperstown, New York, under founder General Abner Doubleday. "It certainly appeals to an American's pride to have had the great national game of Base Ball created and named by a Major General in the United States Army," Spalding said, in certifying the findings. This version of baseball history, which has been passed down through generations, was later proven false.

In fact, historians now think that baseball did develop from the English game of rounders. The modern version of rounders is played on a five-sided field with four posts at the corners. Batters hit a thrown ball with a short bat and then run to each post while the other team tries to get them out. A game called town ball developed out of rounders in New England in the early nineteenth century, and baseball soon evolved from town ball in New York City. Alexander Joy Cartwright, a bank teller, was the organizer of the group that, in 1845, wrote the first set of rules for the game of baseball.

EXPANSION INTO OTHER SPORTS

While baseball was Spalding's main business, he questioned whether his company could continue to grow if it relied solely on that one sport. Searching for new products to add to his line, he discovered that tennis was growing in popularity. During the 1880s, his company began producing tennis balls and racquets. In talking with his customers, he discovered that players tended to be far more concerned with the quality of their racquets than with the quality of the tennis balls. To Spalding, that meant he was better off concentrating his exacting quality control process on racquets. In the 1890s, Spalding applied the same logic to golf. Instead of producing golf balls, he concentrated on being the first U.S. company to design and manufacture golf clubs.

Spalding did not regard other sports as competitors to his beloved baseball; in his view, enthusiasm for one sport led to enthusiasm for all sports. Therefore, in the latter part of the nineteenth century, his company added footballs to its line.

One of Spalding's most lucrative new products came from a totally unpredictable source. In 1891, Dr. James Naismith, an instructor at the YMCA Training School in Springfield, Massachusetts, contacted Spalding with a strange request. Naismith had been toying with a new sport to help athletes keep in shape between the football season in the fall and the baseball season in the spring. The object of the game, said Naismith, was to throw a ball into a box placed high off the ground. The ball that

A modern Spalding football

James Naismith held his first trial basketball game in December 1891, while Spalding was in the process of designing a ball to Naismith's specifications. The players found a soccer ball to use and sent a janitor to find the 15-by-15-inch boxes that Naismith requested for the goals. Unable to find such boxes, the janitor returned with two half-bushel peach baskets, from which the game got its name, basketball.

Naismith requested had to be larger than a baseball so it was easy to see, yet much softer so the players could throw it around at fairly close quarters without getting hurt. Knowing Spalding's reputation for exacting standards in sports equipment, Naismith turned to him to design a ball for his sport, which became known as basketball. Spalding agreed and thus designed the first basketball. Again, he was rewarded for his foresight in taking on a pioneering project. The official rules of the new sport of basketball stated, "The ball made by A. G. Spalding & Bros. shall be the official ball."

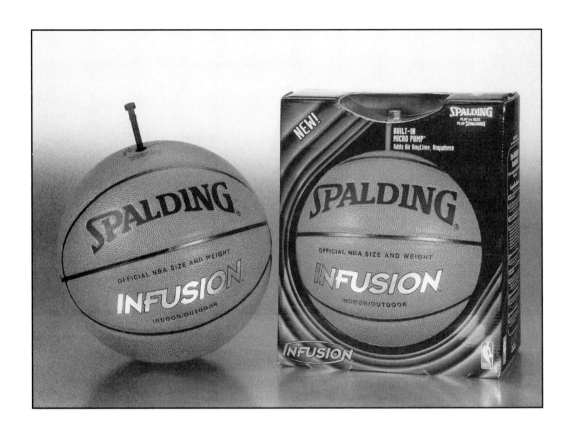

Spalding basketballs continue to be the official ball of the National Basketball Association and the Women's National Basketball Association.

THE CELEBRITY ENDORSEMENT

Having experienced firsthand the advantages a celebrity could give to a fledgling business, Spalding constantly looked for ways to use the public's fascination with sports stars to promote his own products. By the 1890s, many baseball fans were no longer familiar with Spalding's career. So he tapped into the current popular athletes by paying them a fee to use and evaluate his sports equipment. Spalding incorporated their suggestions into his products and then advertised the items as being designed by a Sports Advisory staff of well-known experts.

Spalding took his celebrity connection a step further by going to a star player and offering to custom-design a bat or glove to the star's exact specifications. In exchange for this service and an endorsement fee, the player's name would appear on the product. Spalding's bats and gloves were all inscribed with autographs from the stars who endorsed them.

Kobe Bryant of the Los Angeles Lakers is a modern celebrity endorser. Here he promotes the Infusion basketball, the first basketball to come with a built-in air pump.

This sales strategy proved a great success as many customers, particularly youngsters, wanted to buy the equipment recommended by their favorite players. Spalding then carried the idea yet another step further by persuading star athletes to lend their names to his line of smaller gloves and bats marketed to very young players. Although the celebrities obviously did not use this beginner's equipment, the fact that they recommended it carried great weight with the public.

LATER CAREER

Although he had established his company as the leading manufacturer of sports equipment in America by the end of the century, Spalding never stopped looking for ways to increase business. After concentrating on the manufacturing end of the business for a couple of decades, he took a hard look at his sales situation. He had only three stores in 1899; the bulk of his products were sold to other stores, which then sold them to the public. Spalding decided to develop more fully the retail side of his business. He quickly expanded to 14 stores in carefully selected markets around the country, and the company's profits soared.

Everything ran so smoothly that Spalding decided to retire from the day-to-day operations in the early 1900s, although he continued to keep an eye on the business. His wife, Josie, had died suddenly in 1899, and Spalding remarried shortly after retiring. His second wife, Elizabeth, was a member of a Far Eastern religious group known as the Raja Yoga

Theosophical Society, and she persuaded him to move to southern California, where the society was based, and become a member. Although he was never as enthusiastic as his wife, Spalding would remain a member of the society for the rest of his life.

In 1910, friends persuaded Spalding to run for a U.S. Senate seat in California. He lost the nomination and then faded out of the public eye, spending his time in Point Loma, California, where he died on September 10, 1915.

Albert Spalding playing golf with his wife, Elizabeth (left), near their California home. Spalding's first wife, Josie Keith, whom he had married in 1875, died in 1899. He had no children from either marriage.

Spalding's personal legacy as a baseball player was fixed when, in 1939, he was elected to major-league baseball's Hall of Fame. Equally important was his role in establishing baseball as the national pastime. Not only was he one of America's first professional sports stars, but he was also instrumental in building the popularity of the game.

As a businessperson, Spalding deserves credit for helping to elevate organized outdoor competitive games to a position of major importance in society. He was one of the first in the nation to manufacture and sell sporting equipment, and he was certainly the most successful over the long term. By manufacturing his products to demanding specifications, Spalding won the trust of many of the top sporting organizations. Spalding's baseball was the official major-league ball for over a century, and the company continues to make the official balls for the National Basketball Association and the National Football League Players Association. The company, now known as Spalding Sports Worldwide, remains a leading competitor in the industry. Still headquartered in Chicopee, Massachusetts, it employs more than 1,500 people. Over its 125 years of existence, the company has gradually expanded its emphasis from baseball and basketball to other sports, including soccer and golf, and added active wear clothing to its list of products.

Perhaps Spalding's greatest influence has been his idea of using endorsements from well-known

Professional golfer Len Mattiace uses Spalding's Strata line of balls and clubs. Spalding made the first American golf ball, and golf equipment is now the company's biggest seller.

Examples of Spalding's line of active wear

athletes to sell products. This strategy has been copied by virtually every sporting-goods dealer since, as well as many companies whose products are only remotely related to sports, if at all. The success of such a sales method is clear: companies today consider it well worth their while to pay millions of dollars to star athletes such as Michael Jordan and Tiger Woods to endorse their products.

3

JOSHUA LIONEL COWEN

THE LIONEL COMPANY AND THE TOY TRAIN

Joshua Lionel Cowen was a big talker. He claimed to have been ahead of his time, inventing the doorbell, the dry-cell battery, the electric fan, and the flashlight. When he talked about the train products that made him famous, Cowen made them sound like the greatest pieces of human engineering and manufacturing ever devised. "Why shouldn't a man run a train?" he asked readers in his advertisements. "Why, operating a good train layout is one of the greatest challenges I know!"

The combination of Cowen's inventive mind and his outrageously self-confident marketing drove him to the top of the United States toy industry. For

Joshua Lionel Cowen (1877-1965) combined a love of trains and all things electric with marketing ability to create Lionel toy trains.

nearly half a century, the image of a father and son playing with their Lionel trains stood as one of the most recognizable symbols of American home entertainment.

GROWING UP WITH TRAINS

Joshua Lionel Cohen (he changed his name to Cowen in 1910) was born in New York City on August 25, 1877, the eighth of nine children of Polish immigrants. His father made a comfortable living through his work as a cap manufacturer and part-time real-estate broker. Young Joshua was constantly asking questions and trying to figure out how things worked. His curiosity often got him into trouble—for example, when he broke open the heads of his sisters' expensive porcelain dolls to find out what made their eyes move.

Like many people of the time, both young and old, Cowen was fascinated by trains, which had emerged as the best method of land transportation in the late 1800s. Cowen claimed that he made his own toy train at the age of seven. He also reported that he ruined the wallpaper in one room and nearly scalded himself when the same train, which was powered by a steam alcohol burner, blew up. When Cowen was 12, his family moved to the outskirts of New York City, one block from the tracks of two railroads. There he watched in awe as the smoke-puffing locomotives regularly hauled enormous loads of freight down the iron track.

In 1910, Joshua Cowen changed his name from Cohen to Cowen, possibly to get away from anti-Semitism in his business (although he never hid the fact that he was Jewish) or possibly as "an expression of his Americanism," said Ron Hollander, Cowen's biographer.

ELECTRONICS WIZARD

Although he was an average, often inattentive student in most subjects, Joshua Cowen came alive whenever the topic turned to electricity. He especially enjoyed tinkering with electronics at his high school, the Peter Cooper Institute, where he claimed to have invented the first doorbell. Cowen's inability to concentrate on subjects other than electricity caused him problems after high school. Beginning in 1893, when Cowen was 16, he made three attempts at college, twice at the College of the City of New York and once at Columbia University, but dropped out each time.

Eventually, Cowen found a job at the Acme Electric Lamp Company in Manhattan, where he was able to refine his electronics skills and utilize new resources for his tinkering. He grew interested in batteries, which at that time were all wet-cell batteries, filled with acid. While working at Acme, he claimed to have invented the dry-cell battery, which eliminated the need to use acid in batteries. "I put together one of the first dry-cell batteries ever seen in this country," he said, "but I couldn't make it last for more than 30 days. The materials were lousy."

Many of Cowen's invention claims are impossible to verify because he neither patented nor developed them. He did file a patent claim on June 6, 1899, for what he called the "Flashlamp," a device that used dry-cell batteries to heat a wire fuse to a high temperature. The wire then ignited flash powder, a substance normally used by photographers to

wet-cell battery: a setup that utilizes wire, lead plates, and jars of acid to generate low voltage electricity

dry-cell battery: a battery that produces electricity using an outer case of zinc (negative pole) filled with a paste of chemicals and a carbon rod in the middle (positive pole)

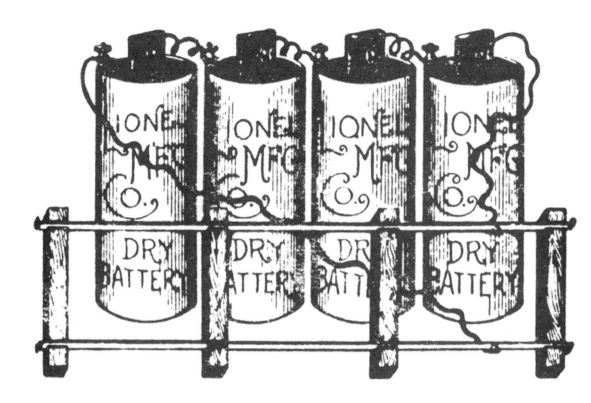

The dry-cell battery was a big improvement over the complex wet-cell battery, which required wires that ran through containers of highly corrosive acid. Electricity from an outlet traveled through the wires to lead plates in the acid.

When asked why he named his company Lionel, Cowen replied, "Well, I had to name it something."

provide light for their subjects. This invention worked well enough that the U.S. Navy contracted with him to produce Flashlamps as a means of detonating mines. A short time later, Cowen obtained a second, similar patent for Electric Explosive Fuses.

By 1900, with the money he'd earned from his navy contract, Cowen was ready to go into business for himself. On September 5, 1900, he and a coworker from Acme, Harry Grant, formed the Lionel Manufacturing Company, the title coming from Cowen's middle name. They manufactured a number of small electrical products, most of which they designed themselves. Cowen constantly experimented with new products, particularly those that could be powered by batteries. He enjoyed telling the story of one invention. When he was looking for relief from one hot New York summer, he attached some blades to a shaft and hooked the contraption up to an electric motor, creating the first electronic fan. Although the motor performed well, the blades produced almost no air circulation and Cowen moved on to new projects, rather than developing the fan.

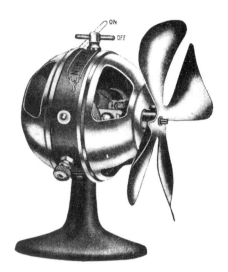

COWEN'S WINDOW DISPLAY

Cowen's search for new ways to use small, battery-operated motors led him to consider making a small electric railway car. Aware of people's fascination with electrical and mechanical devices, he thought a car whirring around in continual motion would be an ideal window display for attracting the interest of passersby. He and Grant built a simple wooden railroad car and then laid a metal track held together by wooden ties.

"It was the most beautiful thing you ever saw. It ran like a dream and it had only one thing wrong with it. You could stand a foot away from the thing and not feel any breeze."
—Joshua Cowen of his electric fan

In 1901, Cowen sold his window display car to Robert Ingersoll, the owner of a toy and novelty shop in New York City. The next day, Ingersoll informed Cowen that he needed more of the cars. The first customer who had been drawn into the store by the display was not interested in any of Ingersoll's goods; he wanted only the electrical car. Ingersoll ordered six more. Soon, other shops in the area followed suit. Customers were buying the display cars for their own use. Instead of having developed a brilliant new advertising idea, Cowen discovered that he had built a popular toy. When a

ties: the wooden beams laid across the bed of railroad tracks to support the rails

store owner in Rhode Island put in an order for 25 display cars, Cowen realized that he was onto something big.

GOING INTO BUSINESS

In order to fill the demand, Cowen scrounged around for scrap metal and wood and set up production in an abandoned loft in Manhattan. The faster he built the cars, the faster the orders came flooding in. Cowen was pleasantly stunned when he sold 22,000 electrical cars in his first year. Building upon his initial success, he added a more ornate and expensive metal trolley to his line and subcontracted its production to Morton E. Converse & Company in Massachusetts. Recognizing that the sale of his railroad car could lead to the sale of other railroad items, he introduced a two-foot suspension bridge as his first option item in 1902.

The Lionel catalog described the first suspension bridge as "an exact reproduction of the suspension railroad bridges to be found all over the country." It sold for $1.50 and had to be assembled.

One of Cowen's most pressing concerns was improving the power source for his electrical toys. If his first cars were popular using the awkward acid-filled wet batteries, he could scarcely imagine what the demand would be if he found a cleaner, easier-to-use source of power. Many potential customers were concerned that the cars were not safe, especially for youngsters. In 1902, Cowen took a step toward eliminating this concern by offering large dry-cell batteries for sale alongside his car. Four batteries could provide between 10 to 15 hours of power.

After obtaining a better power source for his products, Cowen had to improve their appearance. In 1903, he and Grant came out with a new electric car that was actually based on a train engine. Instead of using a steam locomotive, which would have required more complex details, Cowen based his new car on an electric engine. The car was painted

A later Lionel train engine and car carefully replicated from existing trains

Toy manufacturers had been selling self-propelled trains for well over half a century before Cowen's time, beginning with models powered by windup clockwork mechanisms. Cowen himself had played with steam-powered toy trains. As for an electrical component to toy trains, New York blacksmith Thomas Davenport had put together his own model electric train in 1835. German toy maker Georges Carette and Company had delighted crowds at the 1893 Columbian World's Fair with its electric train exhibition. A few expensive miniature electric trains had even been sold commercially in the United States since 1896.

with enamel and had "No. 5" imprinted on its side. It was a first step toward a toy train set.

As Cowen assessed his competition, he realized that he would have difficulty matching the precision and detail of the major German toy train manufacturers. But he believed that most people's fascination with trains lay not in the details but in realistic, powerful motors. He also believed that the public would be willing to sacrifice some of the craftsmanship of the German models in exchange for a larger, reasonably priced train. In its early years, therefore, the Lionel Company concentrated more on improving the technology of its toys than on their appearance.

In 1902, Cowen put out his company's first catalog, a modest, black-and-white, 16-page booklet that was nowhere near as exciting as other companies' "wish books," as they were called. But Cowen would later make up for this first subdued catalog by using a brash concoction of folksiness, pep talk, outlandish boasting, and hard-sell marketing. By 1909, Cowen claimed that his trains were "the standard of the world." He openly derided his competitors' products as worthless pieces of junk and cheap imitations of his quality merchandise. This later hard-line advertising was more in step with Cowen's own personality than the modest 1902 catalog.

TECHNICAL IMPROVEMENTS

During the early years, Cowen spent much of his time on the road, handling the sales end of the business. It was a difficult way to start family life for Cowen, who married Cecelia Liberman in 1904.

Grant was left to handle the administration of the factory, but his expertise lay in inventing, not running a business. Both he and Cowen were relieved when Cowen found Mario Caruso, initially hired as a welder, to be the sort of detail-oriented, no-nonsense taskmaster the factory required. By the end of 1905, the company showed a handsome $8,000 in sales—10 times what they had been in 1901.

In 1906, Cowen made a flurry of technical improvements that paved the way for future success. The most important was a transformer that turned 110-volt household electricity into 20- or 30-volt current, allowing Cowen's trains to run without batteries and without heating up too quickly. Children could also now control the speed of the train. That same year, Cowen introduced a third rail on his track, which helped stop the electrical short-circuiting that sometimes put the trains out of action. In marketing this new track, Cowen pulled off one of the most outrageous public-relations triumphs in the history of American business. His new track was 2⅛ inches in width, as opposed to the 2-inch wide tracks used by other train manufacturers. Yet, despite the fact that he was a much smaller company than his rival train manufacturers, Cowen had the nerve, in the 1909 catalog, to call his track "standard gauge." Calling it that apparently made it so in the public's mind. People referred to Cowen's track as standard gauge so often that competing manufacturers had to switch to Cowen's size train to satisfy their customers.

The Lionel Company's 1902 catalog

Even when other toy train manufacturers switched their gauge size to match Lionel's standard gauge, they still couldn't call their track standard gauge because Lionel had a copyright on the phrase.

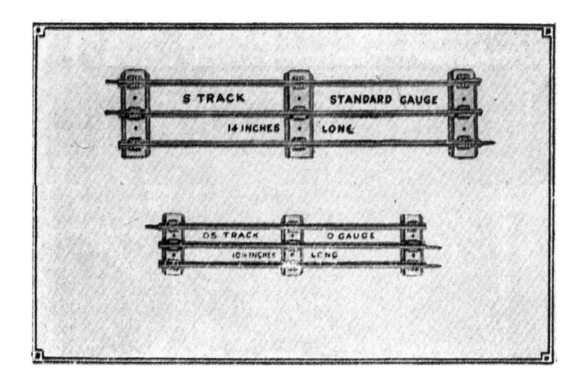

Cowen's standard-gauge tracks. Gauge is the width between the outside rails of a train track. The most popular gauge for model trains today is 5/8 of an inch.

German Competitors

Cowen gained an edge on his competitors by buying materials years in advance when he found a good price. Before long, he was able to sell trains that were larger, more reasonably priced, and more high-tech than his competitors' trains. In 1910, the Lionel Company's sales were up to nearly $57,000, a great deal of money for that time.

Yet despite this success, Lionel continued to lag behind the larger, more established toy train manufacturers. The German companies who dominated the market paid no attention to him, focusing their efforts on outselling W. & S. B. Ives in the United

States. After years of research and development, the German company Marklin prepared an aggressive sales campaign in 1912, featuring the finest, most advanced train set ever produced. Its plans for expansion, which posed a serious threat to Lionel, were derailed in 1914 by World War I. With Germany deeply embroiled in the conflict, its toy train manufacturers suffered. Their factories and materials were diverted to produce weapons for the war effort. American toy stores and their customers who were used to buying toy trains from German companies had to get along without them. This temporary absence of their main competitors allowed young U.S. toy manufacturers, such as Lionel, to capture what was left of the market in wartime. At the same time, Lionel picked up lucrative government contracts for manufacturing compasses and navigational equipment for the war.

When the war ended in 1918, Lionel had managed to capture many of the German companies' former customers. Even when restrictions on German imports were lifted, lingering resentment of Germany kept imports low. The now widespread use of electricity also contributed to Lionel trains' popularity. Lionel, reorganized as the Lionel Corporation, emerged from the decade with sales 15 times larger than when it had started. The company went on to top $2 million in sales in the 1920s.

THE RELENTLESS ADVERTISER

Lionel continued to prosper in the 1920s, fueled by Cowen's innovative, relentless use of advertising.

The company was one of the first U.S. businesses to blanket the nation's media with ads, which appeared in major newspapers, boys' magazines, and the *Saturday Evening Post*. (Many other companies advertised only regionally.) Cowen hired top artists to make his catalogs some of the most colorful and beautifully illustrated pieces of advertising ever produced. He even started a Lionel radio show.

Cowen's marketing message was always personal and energetic. "Twenty years ago I started to make Lionel electric trains for you boys to play with—and NOW—over 550,000 sets are in daily use," he boasted. "Are you one of the lucky thousands?" Cowen played heavily on the angle that trains were both an educational and an intergenerational product. He implied that many railroad men owed their jobs to the early training in technology they had received by playing with Lionel trains and suggested boys would be smart to follow their example. He also appealed directly to fathers, touting his trains as "Real enough for a man to enjoy—simple enough for a boy to operate."

Unable to compete with Lionel's aggressive marketing strategy, W. & S. B. Ives went bankrupt in the mid-1920s. Lionel nearly suffered the same fate when the Great Depression of the 1930s caused a drastic slump in sales. Despite the company's troubles, Cowen refused to cut his employees' wages. The company was saved by several new products, including its new streamlined version of trains (which followed the trend toward streamlining of real trains) and a scale model of the latest diesel

depression: a period of drastic decline in business production and of high unemployment

scale model: a small copy of an object made in proportion to the real object, using the same relationship throughout

engine of one of the most popular railroads in the United States, the Union Pacific. Sales of a Mickey and Minnie Mouse handcar were also brisk. Lionel was showing a profit again by 1935.

GLORY YEARS AND THE SEEDS OF DECLINE

In 1939, Lionel discontinued its standard gauge in favor of smaller, cheaper models. Following World War II, during which Lionel converted its factory to building compasses and cases for the war effort, this smaller line brought the company almost a decade of record sales.

Even during the peak years, however, the seeds of Lionel's decline were beginning to take root. The automobile was rapidly taking over as the nation's dominant form of transportation. Customers became more interested in fast model racing cars

Minnie and Mickey helped pump up Lionel's profits during the 1930s.

than in the old-fashioned train. Ironically, Lionel had tried to market a line of racing cars in 1912, but the concept had been too far ahead of its time. As the era of the train ended, even those people who remained interested in trains turned increasingly to miniature scale-model railroading, with its attention to intricate detail.

Despite record sales in 1953, which made it the nation's largest toy company, the Lionel Corporation was already doomed. It had no solid line of products in reserve to take up the slack. Its attempts to compete with A. C. Gilbert's science and construction kits failed, as did its clumsy attempt to market a line of pastel-colored trains to broaden its targeted customer base to include girls. Between 1953 and 1955, the company's sales plunged 30 percent. Following Cowen's retirement in 1958, the company never again made a profit on its electric trains.

In 1959, Cowen sold his stock in the company to Roy Cohn, a distant relative. Joshua Lionel Cowen died on September 8, 1965, at the age of 88. His death spared him the pain of seeing the company that he founded file for bankruptcy in 1967.

LEGACY

Through a convoluted series of purchases and financial maneuvering, Cowen's Lionel Corporation has survived. In 1969, the company licensed its train manufacturing to General Mills and existed as a holding company specializing in toy stores. In 1985, after a disastrous attempt to relocate its production facilities to Mexico, General Mills sold the Lionel product line

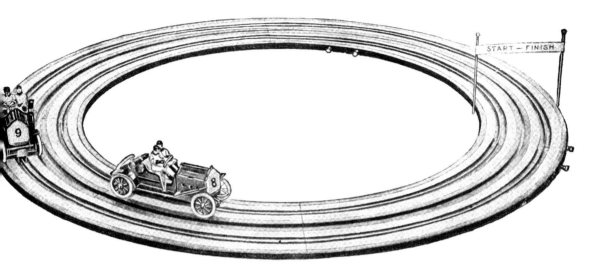

to Kenner-Parker. Kenner-Parker, in turn, sold it to Detroit investor Richard Kughn, who in 1995 sold it to Wellspring. While the company continues to produce trains, it has long since ceased to be an important player in the American toy industry.

From World War I until the late 1950s, however, Lionel trains were the dominant toys in the United States, especially among boys. The trains served as a bridge between generations and promoted family togetherness by allowing fathers and sons to share in play. Joshua Cowen understood the dynamic at work in this type of play, and he pioneered and perfected techniques of advertising that exploited it. His expertise led to sales of more than 600,000 engines and 2.5 million rail cars in 1952 and revenues that exceeded all his rivals. From the humble beginnings of a single demonstration train, Cowen built his one-product company into the largest toy company of his time.

Lionel's racing cars, introduced in 1912, operated by picking up electricity from the groove in the middle of the track. The catalog touted the realism of the cars when "racing, neck and neck, one now forging ahead, and the other striving to overtake it."

revenue: income from an investment, business, or property

4

RUTH HANDLER

MATTEL AND
THE BILLION-DOLLAR DOLL

Barbara Handler has one of the most famous names in the world. Yet, even though millions of girls throughout the world have grown up playing with the product named after her, very few people know who she is or that she even exists.

Barbara was dressing paper dolls one day when her mother realized something unusual about her daughter's play. Barbara did not pretend to be a mother taking care of babies, as was the expected play pattern with dolls. Instead, she always chose grown-up dolls that allowed her to imagine a variety of adult roles. Figuring her daughter knew more than the supposed experts about what little girls wanted, Ruth Handler created a plastic fashion-model doll and named the new toy Barbie, after her daughter.

Ruth Mosko Handler (1916-2002) cofounded Mattel, the largest toy company in the U.S., with her husband Elliot Handler. She created Mattel's most successful product—the Barbie doll.

Ruth Handler's insight into her daughter's play produced the most dramatically successful toy in history. Whereas the Lionel train reigned as the king of boys' toys for several decades, the Barbie doll has flourished as the queen of girls' toys for nearly half a century and shows no signs of slowing down.

SETTLING IN HOLLYWOOD

Ruth Mosko was the youngest of 10 children, born on November 4, 1916, to a family of Polish immigrants who had settled in Denver, Colorado. After graduating from East High School, Ruth startled her family by enrolling at the University of Denver. At the time, few women attended college and Ruth's family gave her little encouragement.

In 1936, after completing two years at the university, Ruth drove with a girlfriend to Los Angeles for a vacation. There she visited another friend who worked at Paramount Studios in Hollywood. Ruth found the glamour of the movie industry irresistible. Although her friend warned her that it was impossible to walk in and get hired at Paramount, Ruth did just that. By the end of the day, she had a job as a stenographer (a person who can write and transcribe shorthand). In 1938, Ruth married Elliot Handler, whom she had dated in high school. Elliot had moved to California to attend art school and be near Ruth. He became an industrial designer and, not long after their marriage, struck out on his own, starting a giftware and plastic costume jewelry business. Ruth would take time off from Paramount to sell Elliot's products.

One day Zachary Zemby, who made items for jewelers, walked into Elliot's shop and asked if they could be partners. Zemby admired the costume jewelry pieces Elliot made. They named the new business Elzac, and Elliot hired his friend Harold "Matt" Matson to run manufacturing. The cash and help Zemby brought came just in time for the Handlers, as their daughter Barbara was born a few months later in 1941.

For the next several years, which included the birth of a second child, Ken, Ruth stayed home to raise her family. Then in 1944, Matson quit after a disagreement with one of the additional partners Zemby had brought into the business. Matson wanted to make some plastic items based on Elliot's old designs. Ruth was eager to lend her business expertise to the venture. "If you make them, I'll sell them," she offered.

MATTEL

Matson put together some samples of plastic picture frames. Ruth took the samples to the manager of a chain of photography stores, who liked them well enough to put in a large order. The Handlers and Matson celebrated their success by forming a new company, which they called "Mattel," a combination of Matson's and Elliot's names.

The very next day, as Ruth was driving in their car, she heard a radio news flash announcing that, because of the military's need for plastic during World War II, it would no longer be available for civilian use. The new company had no choice but to switch to wood for its picture frames.

After the founding of Mattel, Elliot continued to work at Elzac. Sales of Elzac products grew during Mattel's early days, but Elliot was also tired of the interference from Zemby and the other partners. He sold out and joined Mattel full time—and just in time. The creative Elliot could not see letting the leftover wood from the frame construction go to waste. He and Matson began making dollhouse furniture out of it. Eventually, the dollhouse furniture sold so well that Mattel steered away from picture frames and into the toy business. In addition to its furniture, Mattel sold novelty toys, many of them musical toys, such as a plastic ukelele. One of its products was a music box invented by a Hollywood music arranger. It consisted of a rubber belt with carefully positioned knobs that plucked a set of wires when the belt was moved by a crank.

THE TELEVISION GAMBLE

Although Matson dropped out of the business venture in 1947, Ruth and Elliot kept the Mattel name. Sales grew so rapidly that, within a few years, the company was selling over a million dollars' worth of merchandise. In the 1950s, Mattel's growth moved from steady to spectacular, thanks to the Handlers' bold marketing decisions. During its first decade of business, Mattel had been selling through the standard toy outlets of the time—factory representatives, wholesale distributors, and store owners. But when Walt Disney started a daily television show called *The Mickey Mouse Club* in 1955, the Handlers decided to risk their entire business on a costly, untested strategy. They would market their products directly to children via television. Mattel spent a huge amount of money to sponsor a 15-minute segment every week for a year on *The Mickey Mouse Club*.

Many industry experts warned that this was a major blunder. According to their analysis, advertising campaigns for toys proved effective only when directed at adults and when placed during the weeks before Christmas when adults were looking for toys to buy as gifts. But Mattel instantly proved such conventional wisdom wrong. It began by advertising a new Burp Gun, ending its commercials with the catchy slogan, "You can tell it's Mattel; it's swell!"

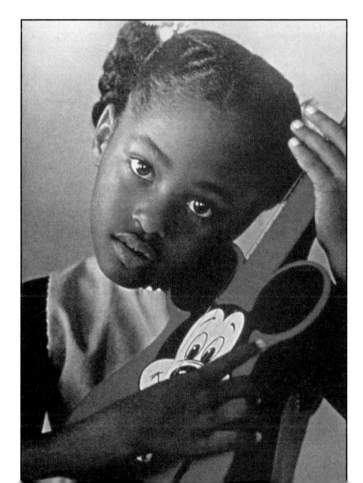

Ruth Handler called the Uke-A-Doodle plastic ukelele Mattel's "first smash hit."

Within six weeks of the advertising campaign, Mattel was flooded with orders. The same thing happened when it aired ads for its new smoking cap gun. The business generated from advertising on children's television shows nearly tripled Mattel's sales in three years, from $5 million to $14 million. Even more importantly, it established Mattel as a recognized name in toys throughout the nation.

A similar defiance of the experts helped Mattel launch the most successful commercial toy product in history in 1959. That was the year Ruth Handler came out with an innovation that revolutionized the doll industry.

INTRODUCING BARBIE

During years of watching her daughter Barbara play with paper dolls, Ruth Handler was intrigued by the way her daughter pretended that the dolls were young women. Sometimes the dolls were college students, other times career women. Noticing that there were no three-dimensional grown-up dolls on the market, Handler decided in 1956 that she would create one.

Handler did not actually design the stiff plastic dress-up figure that she named after her daughter. Borrowing some ideas from a German dress-up doll that she and Barbara had seen on vacation in Switzerland, she outlined the basic specifications that she wanted and assigned her technical staff to look after the details (although she made the final decisions on everything). She also hired a fashion designer to create a wardrobe for Barbie.

"I was convinced that if I could turn this play pattern with paper dolls into a three-dimensional doll, I could fill a very real need in the life of little girls."
—Ruth Handler.

The Purpose of Dolls

Dolls are among the oldest of toys and have been found in the archeological ruins of many cultures. Dolls were supposed to teach girls to care for an infant. During the nineteenth century, dolls were seldom sold with any clothes because sewing clothes for dolls was considered good practice for girls, who would one day sew for their families.

Around the turn of the twentieth century, U.S. toy companies began to market dolls with a different purpose—companionship and role-playing. With this approach, dolls could be sold to boys, too. Perhaps the most popular of the companion toys was created by a couple who owned a candy store in New York City. When news reports hyped the story of President Teddy Roosevelt taking pity on a cornered baby bear during a hunting trip out West in 1902, Morris Michton capitalized on the publicity. He asked his wife to make a stuffed cloth bear and then, after writing to the president for permission to use his name, advertised it as "Teddy's bear." The Teddy bear was an instant success and, in various forms, has retained its popularity a century later.

The Kewpie dolls of the early 1900s, with their chubby, cherubic faces, rode a similar trend in favor of lovable companion dolls. In 1924, the Effanbee Company developed the Patsy doll, which it advertised as a doll with personality. Patsy grew so popular that the company was able to successfully promote a nationwide Patsy Doll Club in 1932.

Perhaps the most popular single doll of the early twentieth century was one made in the likeness of child movie star Shirley Temple. Despite its high price, the doll accounted for one-third of all doll sales in 1935. Some of the most popular dolls after Shirley Temple and before Barbie were the Betsy McCall and Toni dolls of the 1950s. Both were designed as marketing tools for cosmetics companies.

Many of the dolls before Barbie had childlike faces and bodies, despite their womanly accessories. Chubby-cheeked and flat-chested, the dolls often looked out of place in their wedding gowns and other fashionable attire. With the introduction of Barbie in 1959, that would all change.

Little girls caring for a traditional baby doll

The all-male design staff at Mattel told her that the doll would never sell. They adhered to the traditional concept that little girls wanted to pretend to be mommies, so their dolls should be babies. They were also disturbed by Barbie's very developed figure. But Handler insisted that girls did not dream of

The original 1959 Barbie doll and her accessories. Even the earrings could be taken off and put back on.

being mothers as much as they dreamed of being bigger girls. As she told *The New York Times*, "If a little girl was going to do role playing of what she would be like at 16 or 17, it was a little stupid to play with a doll that had a flat chest."

Mattel introduced its Barbie doll at a toy fair in New York City. Many of the buyers, working on the same assumptions as Handler's in-house critics, saw little future for the doll. But the public's reaction showed that Handler knew what she was doing. More than 350,000 Barbies were sold in the doll's first year. Far from being a quirky fad, Barbie remained popular and sales of the doll continued to escalate far beyond what even Handler could have imagined. Capitalizing on its success, Mattel developed a huge line of accessories for Barbie, including a seemingly endless wardrobe. In 1961, the company added Ken, named after the Handlers' son, as a companion doll. Seven years later, Mattel reflected the growing emphasis on diversity in the culture by adding Christie, Barbie's black friend.

By the mid-1960s, sales of Barbie dolls and products transformed Mattel into the nation's largest toy manufacturer. Within a decade of its introduction, the doll had brought in over a half-billion dollars in sales. Competitors tried to follow the trail that Mattel had blazed, but they were too late. Imitation teen dolls such as Hasbro's Jem and Maxie sat on store shelves while Barbie sold out.

Ken and Barbara, for whom the famous dolls are named, with their parents, Ruth and Elliot Handler

Barbie and her circle of friends: (left to right) Teresa, Midge, Christie, Barbie, and Ken

GOLDEN DECADE

It seemed that whatever Mattel touched in the 1960s turned to gold. Following up on Barbie's success, the company recaptured the traditional baby doll market by putting out a talking doll named Chatty Cathy, which quickly became a classic. In 1968, the company brought out a series of flamboyant, brightly painted miniature cars called Hot Wheels. Again, the new products sold well. But even though these other popular products added to Mattel's profits, it was Barbie that built the company into a giant. The company used its earnings to buy other companies, such as Ringling Brothers and Barnum & Bailey Circus and Western Publishing Company, in the late 1960s and early 1970s.

As the architect of Mattel's success, Ruth Handler achieved a status virtually unprecedented for a woman in U.S. business. She moved up from executive vice president to president to cochair of the board of directors of one of the largest and most recognized companies in the world.

LATER LIFE

Mattel's remarkable run of success turned sour in the 1970s, however. At the beginning of the decade, Handler was diagnosed with breast cancer and had to have her left breast removed. The experience devastated her. "I had lost my self-confidence because I had lost my self-esteem after the mastectomy," she said. "You can't be an executive if you can't lead with confidence."

While Handler was losing her grip on the leadership of the company, Mattel suffered a string of setbacks. In the 1970s, a major Mattel factory in Mexico burned to the ground, and a shipping strike in Asia cut off much of the company's supplies. The company's huge expansion brought mounting debts, and Mattel falsified its records. After the company suffered record losses in 1974, government investigators filed charges of illegal bookkeeping against company administrators, including the Handlers. Charges against Elliot were later dropped, but in 1978, Ruth—unable to face a long trial—pleaded no contest. She received a $57,000 fine, five years of probation, and community service.

The episode ended the Handlers' involvement with Mattel. In the meantime, though, Ruth Handler recovered her self-confidence. After being disappointed by the lack of a suitable prosthesis to substitute for her missing breast, she formed her own company to solve the problem. The Nearly Me company operated successfully for 16 years before Ruth sold it in 1991 to Spenco. At that time Ruth, who had acquired considerable wealth from her Barbie invention as well as her latest company, retired. She died in April 2002.

LEGACY

After losing money on many of its non-toy products, the company that the Handlers founded retrenched in 1984. It closed nearly half of its manufacturing plants, sold off most of its holdings, and went back to being exclusively a toymaker. The

name recognition that the Handlers had established for the company helped its recovery. Although Hasbro overtook Mattel as the world's number one toymaker for a few years in the 1990s, Mattel soon regained the lead.

As ever, Mattel owes its marketing position to the innovative little doll that Ruth Handler created in defiance of the experts. Barbie accounted for one-third of all Mattel sales in 2001. The doll is one of

Ruth Handler in later years, once again in good health and sure of her business ability

those rare toys that has crossed generational boundaries without skipping a beat. The granddaughters of women who played with Barbies now have their own Barbies. Annual sales of the Barbie line have continued to rise from $135 million in 1980, to $700 million in 1990, to well over $1 billion in 2001.

Mattel encouraged girls to dress their Barbie dolls in clothes that career women might wear.

The doll has achieved such status that the average girl in the United States between the ages of 3 and 11 owns eight Barbies. The Barbie phenomenon has long since ceased to be strictly an American sensation. More than two-thirds of the sales of Barbie products now occur overseas. Mattel continues to design about 120 new outfits each year, and the amount of fabric it uses for this makes it the world's fourth largest manufacturer of women's garments.

Ruth and Elliot Handler's legacy, however, has extended far beyond the sales of that one product. When Barbie was introduced in 1959, there were more than 200 doll manufacturers in the U.S. Within 10 years, only 60 remained. Furthermore, 80 percent of all dolls manufactured in 1959 were babies. Thanks to Barbie, that figure plunged to 38 percent in 6 years.

The Handlers also introduced methods of marketing that drastically changed the toy industry. Mattel was one of the first companies to understand how toys reflect the prevailing culture, and it moved to take advantage of this. Its use of television to sell toys directly to children also changed the television industry. As a result, Saturday morning cartoons became vehicles to sell products.

Finally, Ruth Handler helped change the face of corporate leadership, as well as the shape of dolls. During Mattel's early days, she was often the only woman in a meeting room filled with men. Today, although the business world is still not an easy place for women, more than ever before are thriving there.

5

OLE KIRK CHRISTIANSEN

LEGO®: NO LIMITS ON WHAT YOU CAN BUILD

Ole Kirk Christiansen's woodworking shop lost money at an alarming rate during the economic depression of the 1930s. Customers were scarce; no one seemed interested in his wooden toys. Saddled with debts that he could not pay, Christiansen had to turn to his nine brothers and sisters for help. They agreed to cosign a bank loan that provided him enough money to stay in business a while longer. But along with their cooperation came some strong advice: in these tough times, he needed to pay more serious attention to his product line. Although the depression made it difficult to find the construction work that had originally paid the bills, his siblings

Ole Kirk Christiansen (1891-1958) built a huge toy business—and gave millions of children hours of creative fun—with small interlocking building bricks.

urged him to at least "make something more useful than toys!"

Christiansen, however, was stubborn. Although he added a few practical products to his store, such as milking stools and Christmas tree stands, he not only refused to abandon his toy products, but he also added a line of building blocks. Eventually, his stubbornness paid off. Over time, Christiansen's shop developed LEGO® bricks, a type of toy building block so versatile yet easy to use that *Fortune* magazine and the British Association of Toy Retailers voted it the "Toy of the Century."

THE CARPENTER'S SHOP

Ole Kirk Christiansen was born in 1891 in Filskov, a tiny village northwest of the town of Billund, Denmark. When he was only six, his family set him to work earning a living as a shepherd. During the long, uneventful hours of tending sheep, he whittled to pass the time. His interest and skill in working with wood led him to learn the carpentry trade. In 1916, Christiansen felt he had mastered enough of the fine points to start a business. He bought the Billund Woodworking and Carpenter's Shop and set to work building houses, window frames, doors, and furniture for the dairy and potato farmers of this rural region.

When construction work dried up during the Great Depression in the 1930s, Christiansen tried to stay in business by selling small, affordable wood products that everyone needed, such as ladders and ironing boards. In designing these products,

Christiansen often started with scale models. He so enjoyed working with such miniature pieces that he began making wood toys in his spare time. Before long, the Billund Woodworking and Carpenter's Shop was filled with cars, trucks, and animals of his own creation.

But while he was a fine carpenter, Christiansen proved to be a poor salesman. He was not very good at advertising the quality of his work. His shop teetered on the edge of ruin until his brothers and sisters bailed him out. Even with their help, it appeared doubtful that Christiansen could continue to produce toys.

Christiansen's woodworking shop in 1916

Ole Kirk Christiansen held a contest to name his company, complete with a bottle of wine as a prize for the best name. He ended up winning it himself with LEGO Company.

An assortment of early LEGO wooden toys

Eventually, however, Christiansen's toy products began to attract customers. By 1934, he was ready to move full time into the toymaking business. He organized a new company that he called "LEGO," from the Danish phrase *leg godt*, which means "play well." With a handful of employees, including all four of his sons, Christiansen began manufacturing wooden toys to be sold by shops other than his own.

Christiansen's enterprise survived the depression primarily due to his relentless insistence on quality. His son, Godtfred Kirk, found out the hard way that his father was serious when he posted his motto on the wall: *Det beste er ikke for godt* (Only the best is good enough). At the age of 12, Godtfred began working at the factory every other day, alternating with school days. One evening he told his father that he had saved money for the company by skipping the last coat of paint on a batch of toys before sending them to the train station for shipment. Ole told him to get down to the station immediately and retrieve the toys before they were sent out. Godtfred then had to stay up half the night applying the final coat that he had missed.

FROM WOOD TO PLASTIC

Ole Christiansen persevered through another rough period during World War II, when the LEGO factory burned to the ground. His thriftiness helped keep him afloat in such times. Rather than living high when sales were good, Christiansen was adamant that

94

most of the profits be put back into the company. This allowed the LEGO Company to expand while staying clear of debt that would have hindered its ability to rebuild and return to business.

In 1947, the old carpenter made the bold decision that put his company on the path to runaway success. At that time, some companies were experimenting with the newly developed synthetic materials known as plastics. Few people in the toy industry saw plastic as anything more than a novelty material. A Danish toy-trade magazine expressed the prevailing

Christiansen built this new LEGO factory in 1942 after the original shop was destroyed in a fire.

Ole Kirk Christiansen gambled on some new technology, this plastic injection molding machine.

opinion when it said, "Plastics will never take the place of good, solid wooden toys." Although he had worked with wood all his life, Christiansen was willing to consider the possibilities of this new material. In 1947, the LEGO Company was the first toy company in Denmark to buy plastic injection molding machinery.

The LEGO Company's first plastic toy product was a fish-shaped baby rattle. Seeing how easily plastic could be shaped and molded compared to wood, Christiansen began marketing a whole line of plastic products. Among the 200 or so products that the LEGO Company produced during 1949 ⑤ was a plastic toy called the Automatic Binding Brick, a hollow block with four or eight studs on top that allowed it to snap together with other blocks.

The fish baby rattle and Automatic Binding Bricks

"No Limits On What You Can Build"

The LEGO Company's blocks and other plastic products quickly began proving the experts wrong. Plastic was replacing a good many traditional wooden toys. By 1951, the LEGO Company's plastic products were already accounting for as many sales as its wooden line. The company began taking a closer look at plastic blocks as a potential source of vast income. In 1953, the LEGO Company began marketing the blocks under a new name—*LEGO Mursten* (LEGO Bricks)—for which it obtained a trademark the following year.

The company's early ads appealed to parents to buy the bricks as an educational toy. According to the LEGO Company, playing with the bricks would "develop the child's critical judgment, manual dexterity, and ability to think for himself."

In 1955, after making a few refinements of the brick, the LEGO Company launched a major campaign to sell the product by developing 28 sets that included various sizes and shapes of blocks. The product was so successful that the company began marketing it outside of Denmark. Ole Kirk Christiansen's confidence in his product showed when, in 1956, the LEGO Company stunned toy industry experts by setting up a sales company in Germany. Germany was still regarded as the toy capital of Europe, a place where toys were exported, not imported, and where foreign toys were looked down on as inferior.

The 1953 LEGO logo

The idea of an interlocking building block did not originate with Ole Kirk Christiansen. The first such product was probably invented by Charles Crandall of New York, who was also a carpenter who turned his woodworking shop into a toy factory. In 1867, Crandall developed a new kind of children's building block that alternated machine-cut tabs with grooves to form an interlocking "tongue and groove" system. By 1878, he expanded this idea to create 28 different sets of interlocking blocks and jointed figures.

Gilbert and the Erector Set

LEGO bricks have not been the only creative building toys to capture the interest of young engineers. Even before Ole Kirk Christiansen started his carpentry shop, A. C. Gilbert manufactured a more complicated but still very successful construction kit called the Erector set.

Albert C. Gilbert, born in western Oregon, was a gifted, high-energy person. As a young boy, he built his own gymnasium in a barn and organized a firefighting unit among the neighborhood kids. He was a fine student who studied at Yale University and eventually became a medical doctor, as well as an exceptional athlete who won a gold medal in pole vaulting at the 1908 Olympic Games in London.

What Gilbert enjoyed most, however, was energizing young minds through the wonders of magic tricks, engineering, and science. After graduating from Yale in 1909, he joined a friend to form the Mysto Magic company, which sold a variety of novelty items. During a train trip on the New Haven and New York Railroad in 1911, he happened to see steel girders being constructed for an electric railway. The sight inspired him to develop, in 1913, a construction kit that a child could use.

Gilbert was not the first person to think of such an idea. In fact, the British company Meccano had introduced a similar product in 1901 and had recently begun marketing it in the United States. Gilbert, however, added some items never seen before in a construction toy. Along with sets of metal strips that could be joined with screws to form sturdy square girders, his "Erector set" included pulleys, gears, and motors.

The fact that Erector sets sold well for nearly half a century came as no surprise to Gilbert. Expressing the prevailing view of his time that there was a clear distinction between boys' and girls' activities, he explained his success by saying, "I built Erector sets because I know what boys like."

Gilbert constantly tinkered with his Erector sets, adding components that allowed young engineers to construct such things as trucks and even amusement park rides. But in his quest to stimulate young minds, he branched out into other educational toys. His chemical and radio sets, designed by experts in their fields, were popular in the post-World War II era, as was his model train.

Unlike the Christiansens, Gilbert's family was unable to expand upon what he had founded. After Gilbert handed leadership of the company to his son in the late 1950s, the A. C. Gilbert Company began to fade from public view. A. C. Gilbert died in 1961, the last Erector sets were sold the following year, and his company was sold in 1965 to the Gabriel Company.

Random samples of finished LEGO bricks are tested for quality in many ways. This LEGO brick is measured with a micrometer screw. Bricks are also dropped, compressed, and bitten by steel jaws. The company checks to make sure the bricks will retain their color, are the correct size, and have no sharp edges.

Constantly striving to improve the quality of his toys, Christiansen gave high priority to his research and development department. In 1958, this group came through by developing a new method of interlocking called the stud and tube coupling system, which would make LEGO bricks unique. With this improvement, LEGO bricks were far more stable than any other building block system, yet the bricks could still be pulled apart easily. That same year, the LEGO Company introduced sloping bricks, which allowed for a greater variety of play construction, including roofing on buildings.

The LEGO system of construction was now unbelievably versatile. "No limits on what you can build," the company advertised. Mathematicians calculated that just six of the studded blocks of plastic could be connected in 102,981,500 ways.

THE LEGO BRICK COMES OF AGE

Having overseen the development of the product that was to make the LEGO Company famous, Ole Kirk Christiansen died in 1955. Godtfred Kirk, known to family and friends as GKC, took his father's place. Within two years of assuming control, Godtfred

Godtfred Kirk Christiansen working with his father Ole Kirk

found himself faced with the same disaster that had plagued his father—in 1960, the company's wooden toy warehouse was destroyed by fire. He decided it was time to cut ties with the company's history. He ordered the wooden toys discontinued. In fact, Godtfred decided to focus the company's entire production on the plastic brick. While business experts warn that tying a growing company's fortunes to a single product is a recipe for disaster, that is exactly what the LEGO Company did.

Year by year, the LEGO Company increased its presence in consumer markets throughout the world. In 1961, the LEGO brick first appeared in what would prove to be one of its most lucrative markets: the United States. Meanwhile, the company continued to expand and improve its line of LEGO bricks. Wheels were added to the system, allowing children to move beyond building stationary objects to making vehicles. In 1963, the company made a formula change, replacing the main ingredient in the bricks, cellulose acetate, with a plastic called acrylonitrile butadiene styrene (ABS). This produced a durable brick that better held the brilliant colors (primarily blue, yellow, red, white, black, and a sprinkling of seven other colors) that would become a LEGO Company trademark.

The process was now perfected. Bright granules of ABS were heated to 437 degrees Fahrenheit under pressure, which melted the material into a paste. This paste was then injected into molds. The exacting quality control standards installed by Ole Kirk Christiansen remained in place. In order to ensure

The improved LEGO bricks designed in the 1960s

that each brick would bond securely with the others yet could be disconnected easily, every mold had to be cut exactly. A variation from the specified dimensions of less than the thickness of a human hair meant that the mold had to be discarded.

During the 1960s, the company recognized that LEGO bricks were difficult for very young hands to manipulate. In 1969, it introduced a new line of bricks, called DUPLO, that were eight times larger than its standard bricks. Not only did this add the preschool population to the LEGO Company's market, but it also primed the interest of these young children to continue with the traditional LEGO bricks as they grew older.

The LEGO Company went to great lengths to prevent competitors from coming up with cheap imitations of its products. Rather than throw away discarded brick molds and allow for the possibility that some rival might salvage them, the company encased every worn-out brick mold in concrete for use in constructing its new corporate buildings.

CHALLENGES IN MARKETING

In addition to his insistence on quality, Ole Kirk left another rigid standard for his descendants to follow. The LEGO brick, insisted Ole, was to be a peaceful, educational toy. It was to be used for creative play, not promoting or glorifying violence.

His father's directive about creative educational play provided Godtfred with a number of challenges as he led the company's growth in the 1960s. He and his researchers discovered that not all children thrived under the complete absence of boundaries that the LEGO Company provided. Many of them preferred some outside direction. In addition, products that could be tied into a popular theme, such as space stations and medieval castles, were far easier to market than a general building block set. The LEGO Company's competitors were beginning to take advantage of this fact. As a result, in 1966, the LEGO Company began to manufacture kits with instructions for putting together specific, predesigned structures.

Kjeld Kirk Kristiansen (center), Ole Kirk's grandson, and two of his friends play with LEGO Town theme building sets.

For some LEGO brick fans, this strategy was hard to swallow. "In the face of competition," author Gary Cross later wrote, "[the] LEGO [Company] had adapted to the all-pervasive marketing techniques of the noveltymakers, sacrificing its initial educational value." Furthermore, after a great deal of internal debate, the company decided that kits featuring medieval knights were merely historical or fantasy subjects and did not compromise Ole Kirk's stand against violent play.

At the same time, the LEGO Company embarked on a revolutionary marketing strategy of using its product in a series of giant, eye-catching displays. Enormous structures built with LEGO bricks appeared in museums, malls, and toy stores throughout the world. In 1968, the company even created a theme park displaying spectacular examples of creativity with LEGO bricks, along with the usual rides. LEGOLAND park, built near the LEGO Company's home offices in Billund, Denmark, boasted a 1.5-million-piece replica of Mount Rushmore and a 3-million-piece reconstruction of the harbor at Copenhagen that took a team of eight workers two years to build.

LEGACY

The company that Ole Kirk Christiansen started in his carpentry shop has grown into one of the world's largest and best-known toy manufacturers. It is estimated that there are over 300 billion LEGO bricks in existence today, more than 50 for every person on the planet. The LEGO Company has grown into an

Above: The Copenhagen harbor display at LEGOLAND in Denmark. Below: The LEGO Imagination Center, located in the Mall of America, Bloomington, Minnesota, is a popular attraction. The center displays large LEGO people hard at work as well as assembled building sets, and hosts a LEGO building area, where parents and children can rest and play.

international corporation that has manufacturing plants widely spaced throughout the world in the United States, Brazil, South Korea, and Switzerland.

Few locales in the world have been so altered by a single company and product as Billund, Denmark, has been changed by the LEGO brick. The town with a population of roughly 5,000 people has become the international headquarters of the famous toy manufacturer and the site of three of its factories. Despite its location far from any population center, the 25-acre LEGOLAND theme park on the outskirts of town has become Denmark's second-largest tourist attraction—its largest outside of the capital city of Copenhagen.

Ole Kirk would be pleased to know that, despite its enormous growth, the company he founded remains in family hands. In 1979, his grandson Kjeld Kirk Kristiansen became the third generation of the family to assume control of the LEGO Company. (Kjeld's last name was accidentally spelled wrong on his birth certificate.)

On an industry-wide level, the LEGO Company defied the business experts. While other toy companies were trying to increase sales by tying toys into the existing pop culture, the LEGO Company created a product with such imaginative possibilities that it actually shaped the culture. Douglas Coupland of the *New Republic* magazine reported that LEGO bricks have provided an important training ground for creative minds. "I came to LEGOLAND from Silicon Valley, where I had been spending time with scores of highly gifted computer

Godtfred Kirk Christiansen valued his close contact with children. Here in 1966 he observes a child's reaction to the LEGO battery-operated train.

engineers. In meeting these people, it quickly became apparent that every one of them had spent his or her youth heavily steeped in LEGO [bricks]," wrote Coupland.

The LEGO Company was able to establish its unique identity because of Godtfred Kirk's recognition of the brick's versatility. Godtfred saw that adding new shapes and sizes each year would increase, not replace, sales of the original product. His innovative sales strategy of promoting the product through colossal displays and a theme park also proved to be a stroke of genius.

Finally, the LEGO Company demonstrated to the toy industry the importance of both exacting quality control and creative research and development. The company maintains a staff of artistic researchers whose job it is to dream up new and creative ways to use LEGO bricks. Their efforts are largely responsible for both attracting and inspiring the young customers upon whom the LEGO Company's business depends.

At LEGOLAND in Carlsbad, California, guests ride human-sized replicas of LEGO cars, boats, and trains. This boy is driving an Aquazone Waver Racer.

6

HIROSHI YAMAUCHI

LEADER OF NINTENDO'S VIDEO-GAME INVASION

At first glance, the Nintendo Corporation seems the classic example of a new, technically innovative business. The video-game company charged onto the scene in the 1980s and dominated a multibillion-dollar industry. It captured the imaginations of youngsters with games that often left adults dizzy with awe and confusion.

Surprisingly, Nintendo is one of the oldest businesses competing in the entertainment industry. The man who brought the company to power, Hiroshi Yamauchi, did so with an iron fist, like the business barons of a century ago. He had no technical expertise. He did not understand the video games his company produced and had no interest in playing them.

Hiroshi Yamauchi (b. 1927) transformed Nintendo into a global business during his 52 years as president. He retired in 2002.

Hiroshi's great-grandfather, Fusajiro Yamauchi, was an artist living in Kyoto, Japan. In 1889, Fusajiro began selling hand-painted playing cards used in a game called *hanafuda*. He named his company Ninten-do, which means "work hard, but in the end it is in heaven's hands."

At first, Fusajiro's elaborate cards, illustrated with flowers, trees, and animals, were made from the bark of mulberry trees. The cards appealed mainly to upper-class Japanese. But when *hanafuda* became popular with gamblers, business increased because professional players used a new deck at the beginning of each game. After taking the bold step of adding Western-style playing cards to its product line in 1902, Nintendo became the largest playing-card manufacturer in Japan.

Nintendo remained a small, profitable family business when Fusajiro's great-grandson, Hiroshi Yamauchi, was born in 1927, in Kyoto. Hiroshi's father abandoned the family when the boy was five. Hiroshi went to live with his grandparents, who were running Nintendo. He never saw his father again and spent little time with his mother. Life with his strict, no-nonsense grandparents was harsh. Hiroshi grew up sullen and arrogant, without warmth or compassion.

After spending the terrible years of World War II in a Kyoto prep school, Hiroshi went on to Waseda University to study law. But while he was there, his grandfather suffered a severe stroke and asked

Hiroshi to drop out of college and take over the family business. Hiroshi agreed on one cold-hearted condition. Fearful of anyone in the family challenging his authority, he insisted that his cousin who worked at Nintendo be fired. After becoming head of the company, Hiroshi gradually dismissed every manager who had worked for his grandfather, including those who had been faithful employees for decades.

For a long time, Hiroshi cautiously tended the card business. But when business slacked off, he guided the company on a new course by signing its first licensing agreement in 1959. This agreement, which allowed him to use Walt Disney characters on his cards, provided a temporary boost in sales.

SEARCHING FOR A PRODUCT

Yamauchi feared that Nintendo could not survive with playing cards as its only product. As business faltered again in the 1960s, he groped about for other products. With no clear business plan, he sold instant rice, then started a hotel business, and finally ran a taxi service. All failed or proved troublesome to run. Yamauchi took stock of his situation and realized Nintendo's two key assets were a good reputation in the entertainment field and a distribution system that placed his cards into stores. He decided his best chance for survival was to expand within the entertainment field. With that in mind, Yamauchi organized a research and development team in 1969 to create new games and toys.

Yamauchi used no market research, nor did he ever ask for a second opinion. Relying purely on his

Fusajiro Yamauchi had no sons. So when his daughter, Tei, married Sekiryo Kaneda, Kaneda agreed to take the Yamauchi family name and enter the family business of his bride, a Japanese custom. Tei and Sekiryo Yamauchi also only had daughters. Their oldest daughter, Kimi, married Shikanojo Inaba, who, like his father-in-law, took the Yamauchi name and became the next in line to run Nintendo. Their child, Hiroshi, was born in 1927, the first male Yamauchi in three generations. After Shikanojo left his wife and son, Tei and Sikiryo raised their grandson. Hiroshi has a son, Katsuhito, but he is not interested in running the company.

own instincts, he ignored what was currently popular. Instead, he tried to imagine what would be popular 10 years down the road. Nintendo engineers and inventors trembled as they brought their ideas to the gruff, intimidating company head. Would Yamauchi kill their project with a scornful glare, or would he reward them with a nod of approval? As one Nintendo engineer said, employees enjoyed few perks or benefits, but "we lived for his praise."

Hiroshi Yamauchi's instincts proved remarkable. Nintendo enjoyed brief success with original products such as simulated laser guns. During the early 1970s, Japanese consumers flocked to Nintendo's new Beam Gun shooting ranges.

In 1973, however, economic changes affected Nintendo's success. Many oil-producing nations suddenly cut down on how much oil they exported. The shortage caused the price of oil to skyrocket in Japan. Consumers no longer had extra cash to spend at shooting ranges. Nintendo's sales plummeted so steeply that the company nearly went bankrupt. Searching desperately for a new product to save his company, Yamauchi turned to video games.

FROM SPACE WARS TO PONG

Video games as a new form of entertainment originated in the United States in 1962. Steve Russell, a graduate student at the Massachusetts Institute of Technology, spent hours trying to program an early computer to produce dots that changed direction. Finally he succeeded and turned his breakthrough into a game called "Space Wars." By the mid-1970s, a host of new companies, led by Atari, were producing video games that could be played on home television sets.

Yamauchi tried to catch a ride on the new video-game wave that swept the entertainment industry. By 1977, his researchers had developed an entertainment system that could run tennis games similar to the popular Atari game "Pong." Nintendo sold one million of these systems and this kept the company afloat during a rough time.

In 1997, two sisters played an original Pong video game at the Cyber Playground exhibit of home and arcade video games and computers. The exhibit was at the Liberty Science Center in Jersey City, New Jersey.

Bushnell and the Video Game

Nolan Bushnell had a sure-fire idea for a new product in 1971. Noting the popularity of a computer game called "Space Wars" among college students, he designed a coin-operated arcade version of the game, "Computer Space." The Utah-born engineer, working in California, tried to market his new game to arcades as an alternative to pinball. Computer Space, however, was too complicated for the average person. It failed miserably.

One of Nolan Bushnell's ventures after Atari was the Chuck E. Cheese's chain of restaurants that featured pizza and video arcade games.

Bushnell learned from his mistake and tried again with a much simpler game. "To be successful, I knew that I had to come up with a game that people already knew how to play," he said. Working in his basement, Bushnell invented "Pong," in which two players used video paddles to hit a ball past each other. The game required only one instruction: "Avoid missing ball for high score."

In 1972, Bushnell tested his new invention at Andy Capp's Tavern in Sunnyvale, California, where it was an instant hit. Encouraged, Bushnell and a friend scraped together $500 and started a business he named Atari. The company could not keep up with the demand for Pong. In 1973, it shipped 6,000 copies of the video game.

The real breakthrough, however, came when Bushnell developed a system that allowed a person to play Pong on an ordinary television. The convenience of playing a fascinating video game at home sparked a sales explosion. Sears ordered 150,000 Pong sets in 1975, and the game soon became the best-selling item in its catalog.

Although he introduced the video game, which *Variety* magazine called "the first new entertainment technology since the television," Bushnell himself did not last long in the business. As he admitted, "I'm not a very good CEO." Before the end of the 1970s, he sold the company to Warner Communications and moved on to other pursuits.

"THROW AWAY ALL YOUR OLD IDEAS"

Yamauchi recognized that his games were nothing special. In the highly competitive, fast-changing world of video games, new technology would quickly make his current products seem like primitive toys. Nintendo had to do more than come up with gimmicks and variations on what others sold. It needed to leap out far ahead of everyone else. "Throw away all your old ideas in order to come up with something new," Yamauchi ordered his staff.

The first of Nintendo's new creative projects was an attempt to take advantage of the miniaturization of computer technology. In the early 1980s, Nintendo came out with video-game machines the size of a pocket calculator.

But Yamauchi wanted to stretch the limits of video-game technology further. He insisted on more memory, colors, and features for his video machine. Unfortunately, these features required an expensive and complex computer chip called a microprocessor that would push the cost of the machine beyond the range of many consumers. The only way the price could drop enough to be practical was if the supplier mass-produced the chips. Yamauchi risked his company on the idea that he could sell millions of machines powered by this new computer chip. He agreed to buy three million chips from his supplier if it would sell the chips at a discounted rate. Industry experts ridiculed Yamauchi for the move. They were convinced he would be stuck paying for many thousands more chips than he could use.

chip: a tiny electric circuit that may contain millions of electronic parts. Chips store instructions that run computers and process data.

microprocessor: the complex chip that is the central processing unit of a computer

bit: a single-digit number that represents zero or one in computer language and is the smallest unit of computer data, from the term "binary digit"

Nintendo took the new eight-bit microprocessors and created a revolutionary machine. Instead of the standard 6 to 8 colors used in video games, Nintendo's system offered 52. It held almost 10 times the memory of Atari's system. Fearful of scaring off those who found computers intimidating, Nintendo engineers designed a system that was simple and easy to use. It discarded disk drives in favor of a cartridge that the customer popped into the system.

Yamauchi also thought of a clever way to capture the market. He would sell the hardware (the game machine) for little more than the cost of production. Not only would Nintendo's system be superior to anything else on the market, but it would also cost less than half what competitors asked for their systems. That would entice millions of consumers to buy. Once they had purchased the hardware, consumers would demand the software (games). Nintendo would make money by selling the games at a huge profit.

After months of working in secret, Nintendo introduced the Famicom (short for Family Computer) to Japan in 1983. Nintendo sold a half-million in the first two months. But just as Yamauchi was about to celebrate his success, bad news arrived.

integrated circuit: an electronic circuit etched on a tiny chip of germanium or silicon that holds thousands of electronic elements

One of the integrated circuits was causing some of the games to freeze up. Realizing that his daring assault on the video-game market depended on a reputation for quality, Yamauchi immediately recalled all machines to have them repaired. The move cost Nintendo millions of dollars, but it proved

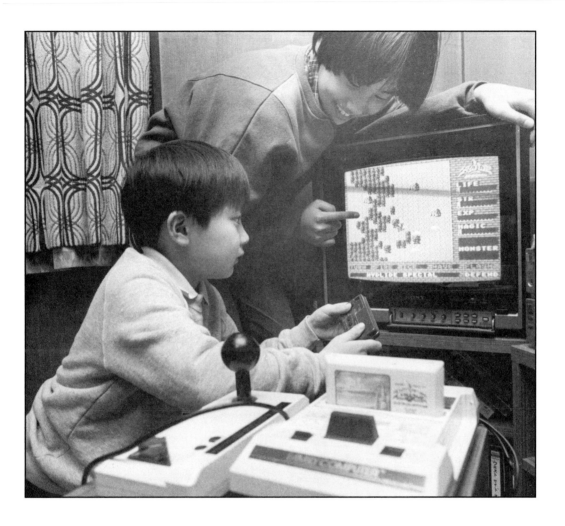

a smart investment. When the fully functioning machines were reintroduced, Nintendo sold them as fast as it could build them.

These children in Tokyo are playing on the Family Computer or Famicom, Nintendo's first game console.

Miyamoto's Creation

Never one to rest on his achievements, Yamauchi kept searching for new games and innovations. Although he tightly controlled all final decisions in the company, he gave his creative artists freedom to explore their own ideas. His best move was to promote a young apprentice artist named Shigeru Miyamoto to the position of game designer in 1980. At the time, others in the company questioned why Yamauchi gave the inexperienced Miyamoto such an important position. But Yamauchi, whose instincts seldom failed, saw something special in the young employee.

Miyamoto disliked the mindless violence of many popular video games. Using the story of Beauty and the Beast as a springboard, he developed a storyline about an ape and a master plumber wearing baggy pants. Miyamoto called the ape Donkey Kong (because the beast was stubborn and resembled King Kong) and the master plumber Mario. Remembering a time in his youth when he was exploring a cave and found yet another cave within, Miyamoto created doors within doors and mysterious paths that led to colorful settings, bizarre creatures, and new adventures.

AMERICAN BREAKTHROUGH

Nintendo had achieved some success in the U.S. by licensing video arcade games to American companies. Yamauchi's daughter and son-in-law, Yoko and Minoru Arakawa, founded Nintendo of America in 1980. Briefly headquartered in New York City, the company soon moved to Seattle. After the success of the arcade version of Donkey Kong, they built new headquarters in Redmond, Washington, not far from the sprawling Microsoft complex.

Believing that his small company could never compete against huge American companies, Yamauchi tried to license the sale of his game machine for the home to Atari. But while the two sides were working out the agreement, Americans lost interest in the video-game fad. Industry sales

Game creator Shigeru Miyamoto has been hailed as the Walt Disney of video games. This creative man has won awards and fans for his memorable characters, including Donkey Kong, Super Mario, and Zelda.

plunged from $3 billion in 1981 to about $100 million in 1983. The crash pitched Atari into a fatal tailspin and it could no longer afford to buy anything from Nintendo. Ironically, this prompted Yamauchi to enter the U.S. market for himself.

Before introducing the Nintendo home game machine into the United States, Yamauchi took a close look at the disastrous American home video-game business. He concluded that lack of control over products had been Atari's fatal mistake. By the time the market collapsed in 1983, more than 1,500 games were available for the Atari system. Most were poorly designed and engineered. Imitators had produced cheap versions of Atari technology, and Atari could not compete.

To avoid these mistakes, Hiroshi Yamauchi kept tight control over the software for the new Nintendo Entertainment System, introduced in 1986. Nintendo designers created most of the games themselves. Any outside software company that wanted to design a game for Nintendo had to sign a licensing agreement highly favorable to Nintendo. Furthermore, Nintendo engineers designed the system to run only those programs that used a patented Nintendo computer chip. Unauthorized games simply would not work on the Nintendo.

Master game designer Shigeru Miyamoto was now a producer, overseeing many projects. When he finished writing the script for a game and painting the main characters, he turned the project over to other artists, editors, programmers, and music composers. He then tested the final product. If portions seemed too easy, he added obstacles; if too difficult, he provided items such as magic mushrooms to help the player.

At first, Nintendo sales managers in the United States hated the Donkey Kong game. They could not believe this whimsical game could compete with the intense action and violence of their competitors' games. One salesman quit in disgust rather than try to sell it. Yamauchi insisted the game would sell. As usual, he was right. Miyamoto's Donkey Kong earned over $200 million in America for the company. The sequels of the adventures of the Super Mario Brothers became by far the best-selling games of their time. Super Mario Brothers 3 would eventually sell seven million copies in the U.S and four million in Japan, making it the best-selling game of all time.

Nintendo took the U.S. market by storm, just as it had in Japan. By 1988, Nintendo's U.S. division had sold 7 million systems and 33 million game cartridges. One year later, Nintendo Entertainment Systems were in use in one out of every four homes in the United States. That figure rose to one of every three homes in 1990. Thirty million households were playing Nintendo games, far more than owned a computer.

By 1989, Nintendo replaced automobile giant Toyota as Japan's most successful company according to the *Japan Economic Journal*. This publication judges companies based on how well they are run, how they perform on the Japanese stock market, and overall profits. Nintendo earned $1 billion in profits

In 1989, Nintendo also introduced Game Boy, the first portable, hand-held game system with interchangeable game packs.

stock market: a place where stocks and bonds are actively traded

Minoru Arakama, president of Nintendo of America, Inc.

in 1991, an incredible amount of money for a company that employed fewer than 1,000 people. Yamauchi kept his costs low by manufacturing nothing himself. He subcontracted production of the actual machines and parts to smaller companies.

Ironically, the man who brought fun to so many millions of consumers reigned over his expanding empire with joyless obsession. He never played the games that his company produced. The only game he ever played was "Go," a traditional Japanese board game. Other than this, his executives claimed, he had no interest in anything but building his company. The walls of the rooms and halls in his office were bare, a tribute to his stubborn insistence that decorations were just useless distractions.

Yamauchi remained aloof, mysterious, and unpredictable. Although he avoided attention most of the time, he created a fuss by purchasing a 60 percent interest in the Seattle Mariners baseball team in 1992. The idea of a foreigner owning a piece of the national pastime outraged many Americans. Although baseball is popular in Japan, Yamauchi did not care for the sport and never attended games. He said that he bought the Mariners to help Seattle, the community in which his American offices are located, keep a professional baseball team.

DEFENDING ITS TURF

Nintendo became so powerful in the industry, and its intimidating leader so feared, that many rejoiced when the company slipped from its perch in the early 1990s. A competitor, Sega, beat Nintendo to the development of a new entertainment system—Genesis—powered by a 16-bit computer chip. This new chip held so much more information that it increased the range of colors in entertainment systems from 52 to 500, offering high-definition graphics, a three-dimensional look, and better sound. Sega launched a blistering advertising campaign that belittled Nintendo's 8-bit machines. The new technology made millions of Nintendo game cartridges seem primitive by comparison.

Nintendo was slow in responding to the Sega challenge. "We allowed Sega to brand our games as children's toys. It was a serious mistake," Yamauchi fumed. From 1992 to 1993, the company's share of the video-game market fell from 60 percent to 37 percent. No sooner did Nintendo begin to meet the challenge with its 16-bit Super Nintendo System than another competitor attacked. Sony jumped in with yet another advance, a 32-bit entertainment system called PlayStation. Again, Nintendo rushed to catch up, but again came in too late. Nintendo's 32-bit Virtual Boy barely made a ripple in the industry.

As before, Yamauchi's answer was to look into the future. He joined with an American partner, Silicon Graphics, Inc., to invent the next generation of computer games. The result, introduced in 1996, was the remarkable Nintendo 64, a 64-bit system with dazzling three-dimensional graphics. Consumer response to these new machines was positive—almost 20 million units had been sold by 2001—although some players thought this system needed more good games.

As one Nintendo executive admitted, "As long as he's the boss, I'll sleep better at night."

As Yamauchi crossed over into his seventies, industry experts speculated as to how long he would continue to rule Nintendo. That question was answered in May 2002 when Yamauchi retired after leading Nintendo for 52 years. Observers wondered if anyone could replace Yamauchi. That question has yet to be answered.

Sega and Sony

Nintendo's main rival, Sega, also traces its history to Japan, although with a distinctly American twist. It was registered in 1951 as Service Games of Japan, or Sega, by Martin Bromely, who had formed the company in Honolulu, Hawaii, 11 years earlier. The company manufactured coin-operated arcade games for U.S. military bases in Japan. In 1965, Sega merged with Rosen Enterprises, Inc., which had been formed by David Rosen in 1954. Rosen then became CEO of Sega. Four years later, the company was sold to Gulf & Western Industries, the first of many ownership changes.

Prior to the 1980s, Sega continued to market primarily to Japan. But in the early 1980s, it expanded into the U.S. market, where it quickly emerged as Nintendo's primary competitor. In 1999, Sega introduced a new game system, Dreamcast, the most powerful video game console to that point. Fired by two central processing units, it offered players superior graphics, surround sound, and a 56K modem for surfing the Internet or sending e-mail messages. Later that same year, the company made online gaming available.

Another Japan-based rival, Sony, seriously challenged Nintendo in the early 1990s with its 32-bit console PlayStation. PlayStation 2, the first 128-bit system, was released in 2000. Sony had sold 30 million units by May 2002.

Sega's Dreamcast game console did not catch on, and the company now focuses on games.

In 1998, Nintendo introduced Pokemon cards, computer games, and cartoon shows. The little Pokemon creatures earned billions for Nintendo during the first year the toys were available. These children are playing in a Pokemon Game Boy tournament.

LEGACY

In taking control of the United States market, Yamauchi accomplished a startling cultural takeover. Never before had a foreign company held such sway over young Americans. By the early 1990s, more children in the U.S. were familiar with Super Mario than with one of the most traditional American icons, Mickey Mouse. Led by Yamauchi's Nintendo, video games surged past television as an influence on children. According to the Toy Manufacturers of America, video games now outsell all other toys, games, and puzzles combined. In 2000, 7 of the 10 top-selling video games in the world were Nintendo products, and the company's industry share had grown to an impressive 48 percent.

By constantly updating its products, Nintendo has managed to stay ahead of its rivals. In 2001, Nintendo introduced the 128-bit Game Cube and broke all previous U.S. sales records. Game Boy Advance, the update of Nintendo's portable game player, also debuted in 2001, and sold one million units in six weeks.

Some argue that video games have had a dangerous effect on young people—turning them into couch potatoes with no drive or interest in more serious pursuits. Others hail video games as simple computers that can give children the skills and understanding necessary to operate more complicated computers as they grow older. Either way, the trend that Yamauchi started shows no immediate signs of fading. The sales figures for electronic games designed for play on consoles and personal computers were higher in 2001 than the total box office earnings of Hollywood movies.

7

GARY GYGAX

DUNGEONS & DRAGONS: GAMES WITHOUT WINNERS

For centuries, the basic feature of games has been competition. Games have traditionally matched one person against an opponent or opponents in a contest to see who can achieve a specific objective. Games have offered a chance for people to match their skill, intelligence, and luck against one another. By their nature, games typically conclude with winners and losers.

In the 1970s, a small group of hobbyists, led by Gary Gygax, changed all that. They invented a game that has no winners or losers and often has no definable ending point. The game is so detailed and complicated that a newcomer cannot possibly begin to learn it except by studying thick manuals or by being personally tutored by experts. In short, their

The original Dungeons & Dragons Master, Gary Gygax (b. 1938) invented a new type of game that has grown into a billion-dollar-per-year industry.

game, according to one game industry executive, "violates all the traditional rules for a successful game." Yet the game they invented, Dungeons & Dragons, became a smash success. The concept behind Dungeons & Dragons proved so original and fascinating that it launched a whole new genre of games known as role-playing games, or RPGs.

WAR GAMES WITH A TWIST

The driving force behind this revolution in leisure activity was Chicago native Gary Gygax, who was born on July 27, 1938. Gary became interested in the world of fantasy through his father, a violinist with the Chicago Symphony, who enjoyed reading fairy tales to his son. As a teenager, Gary found a new outlet for his active imagination in a small but dedicated group of hobbyists whose interest was war games.

Gary Gygax was fascinated by the detail and historical accuracy of war games. He became so obsessed with the games that his studies suffered, and he quit high school after two years. Realizing that a grown man could not spend his whole life playing games, he returned to earn his diploma. In 1958, he married his high-school sweetheart, Mary Powell, and settled in Lake Geneva, Wisconsin, where they eventually had five children. Gygax earned a living working in the office of an insurance company.

The responsibilities of a family, however, did not cause him to completely abandon his love of war games or historical detail. He became especially

role-playing game (RPG): a game in which players act out or discuss scenarios in the role of characters they've chosen or had assigned to them

War Games

War games are among the oldest of games, dating back to the third century B.C. They are basically re-creations of battles or theoretical battle situations, governed by a set of rules that determine a player's success. Some games use miniature action figures as markers, while others have game pieces that represent components of an army. For many years, participation in war games was limited to professional soldiers, who used them to gain experience and expertise in battle situations they might encounter, and historians, who probed for the reasons behind the outcomes of certain battles.

In 1915, however, the noted science fiction author H. G. Wells put together a set of rules for amateur war games players. A small but dedicated group of war gamers emerged, particularly in Western nations. But with its difficult rules and long playing times, the war game genre remained a specialized hobby of only a few dedicated gamers.

In 1953, Charles Roberts attempted to move war games into the commercial game market by designing a board game called Tactics. The public reacted with yawning indifference, though, and Roberts was able to sell only 2,000 copies in five years. He tried again, basing his second war game on a well-known historical event, the Battle of Gettysburg. This time he attracted enough interest that his newly formed Avalon-Hill game company flourished. For the next 10 years, the Baltimore-based company developed and marketed a line of 20 games to war game enthusiasts with virtually no competition. As a result, Avalon-Hill became one of the most well-known names in the war game industry.

interested in medieval warfare and joined a group of like-minded hobbyists called the Castles and Crusades Society. Occasionally, Gygax attended conventions where he met people who shared his interest.

One of those people was David Arneson. In 1968, Arneson was playing a medieval war game with a group of friends in Minneapolis, Minnesota, that had turned dull. To rekindle the participants' interest, one of the friends, who was running the game, gave each of the participants a personal goal in the battle. Previously, each player was simply carrying out general battle strategy. War games were traditionally played under rigid rules based on history and the realities of warfare—there was nothing in the rules that allowed for what the officiator had done. But Arneson enjoyed the twist; it opened his eyes to a realm of possibilities that he had never considered. He began to think about other creative ways to spice up war games.

A short time later, Arneson was officiating a war game set in ancient times, pitting the Romans against the Britons. As he unfolded the battle scene, it occurred to him to give the Britons a Druid with mystical powers. The Roman war elephants charged the Britons, who had no defense against the huge beasts. But as the Romans were about to destroy their enemies, in Arneson's words, ". . . the Druidic high priest waved his hands and pointed this funny little box out of one hand and turned the elephants into so much barbecue meat."

Arneson's fellow players were stunned. The rules of warfare did not account for wizards casting spells that upset the balance of power. But Arneson knew he was on to something. He became intrigued with the idea of a game patterned after war games that included elements of fantasy and magic. In 1970, he organized a game that he called the Blackmoor Dungeon Campaign.

BUILDING DUNGEONS & DRAGONS

Through his and Arneson's common membership in the Castles and Crusades Society, Gary Gygax learned of these ideas. Almost immediately, he began to come up with imaginative ways to play with the concepts that Arneson was exploring. Although they lived in different cities, the two men worked together to design a new game. Each would play-test different ideas and then write to the other,

A Druid from the current Dungeons & Dragons Player's Handbook. *Because Druids gain power from their connection to the natural world, they often have animal companions, or cast spells that involve nature or animals.*

describing what worked and what did not. Gygax, who had been writing rules for war games as a hobby, began to formulate a set of rules. An avid reader of books on medieval society, he had a wealth of knowledge on which to draw for his work. He particularly relied on a book called *Arms and War: The Welsh Wars of Edward I.* In 1971, he coauthored a booklet called *Chain Mail*, a guide to miniature war games and fantasy games. Gradually, a game that Arneson and Gygax called Dungeons & Dragons began to take shape.

The game relied on a player who served as Dungeon Master. This person would create on graph paper (or often just in his or her head) a dungeon filled with treasures, such as gold and magic devices; hazards, such as traps and evil creatures; and puzzles, such as riddles and mazes.

One of the innovations that made Dungeons & Dragons unique was the construction of a detailed personal profile for each player. Much of that profile was constructed through chance, using a character-generating system developed by Gygax and Arneson. Using various dice with 4, 6, 8, 12, and 20 sides, each player would roll to determine the different aspects of his or her character. Degrees of strength, constitution, dexterity, intelligence, wisdom, and charisma were decided by the roll of three six-sided dice. The outcome of these rolls dictated what type of character would best suit the player (for example, high dexterity might make for a good thief; high wisdom, a good magic user).

An Imaginary World

When the characters were set, the Dungeon Master would guide the players on a journey, telling them what they would find as they made various directional choices. Here again, chance played a part in the proceedings, as the characters rolled dice to determine the outcomes of encounters with monsters as varied as gelatinous cubes and dragons. The numbers needed to score a win varied with the

There are two types of dragons in the game. Chromatic dragons are black, blue, green, red, and white, all evil and fierce. Metallic dragons—brass, bronze, copper, gold, and silver ones—are good, but can be as fierce as their colorful cousins. This copper dragon enjoys jokes and riddles.

predetermined traits of the characters. For example, each character could sustain a certain amount of injury from an encounter, measured as "hit points," before he or she died. Hit points could be restored by rest, spells, potions, and wizardly powers. The enormous variation in characteristics and in possible hazards or treasures required Gygax and Arneson to assemble piles of complex charts and tables. These listed such things as odds of survival given different levels of armor, experience, strength, and ability to cast spells. As the characters succeeded in their encounters, they collected treasure and experience points, which would allow them to enter more dangerous and rewarding dungeons.

Although the project started out as a hobby, Gygax began to think about marketing the game. He sent a copy of the rules to two game companies, but both turned him down. Game manufacturers were turned off by two features: the complexity and the open-endedness. Dungeons & Dragons required hours of planning before the game could even start and had rules covering so many possible outcomes that the experts thought players would be hopelessly confused. The lack of a specific goal and end point also bothered the game manufacturers. In Gygax's game, players did not necessarily compete against each other—they could go their own way or team up to help each other. The game had no ending, unless all the players were killed off or agreed among themselves to stop the journey. Gygax explained, "The ultimate aim of the game is to gain sufficient esteem as a good player to retire your character," who then

"This is really the first commercial attempt to provide a game where the players can really use their imaginations and ingenuity freely. If you run into a dragon sitting on a pile of treasure, you can attack it and attempt to slay it. You can try to negotiate with it. You can use trickery. You can back away if you don't think you can handle it, and maybe come back another time."
—Gary Gygax, of
   Dungeons & Dragons

"becomes a kind of mythical, historical figure, some-one for others to look up to and admire." But the real fun of the game was simply in spending some time with friends on an exciting adventure in a make-believe world.

FRONT-PORCH INDUSTRY

The discouraging reception he received from game manufacturers temporarily caused Gygax to pull back in his efforts to market Dungeons & Dragons.

Gary Gygax and friends on a role-playing adventure together

But then, in the early 1970s, he suddenly lost his insurance job. Forced to make a new career choice, Gygax opened a shoe repair shop in the basement of his Lake Geneva house. But at the same time, losing his job security led him to ponder the possibilities of earning a living marketing his creation himself.

Gary Gygax self-published his first version of Dungeons & Dragons. Initially, sales were slow. Using his contacts in the world of medieval war gamers, Gygax managed to sell about 1,000 copies in 11 months. This was enough to spur him into more aggressive action. He and a friend, Don Kaye, pooled their meager resources and came up with $1,000 to form a company they called TSR (Tactical Studies Rules) Hobbies, Inc.

In 1974, Brian Blume, a games enthusiast from Chicago, joined Gygax and Kaye. Accepting that the odds of actually making a living off the game were poor, they ran a shoestring operation in a converted hotel bar and bowling alley. Everyone involved had a full-time job to support himself. "It was a front-porch industry," Gygax admitted. "We did it with a lick and a promise." This occasionally meant corners had to be cut, and the hastily edited original edition included poor grammar and organization.

But in its second year, Dungeons & Dragons showed signs of being a viable product, selling a second 1,000 copies in only three months. Feeling they had survived the perilous start-up months of their new business, Gygax and Blume committed themselves to working full-time at TSR. Fueled by a

TSR Hobbies, Inc., was set up as an equal partnership between Gygax and Kaye. After Blume joined them, the company's equity was divided among the three men. When Kaye died in 1976, Gygax purchased Kaye's third from his widow. Later, Gygax found himself short on cash, so he sold some of his shares of TSR to Blume and members of Blume's family, giving them about 60 percent interest in the company.

tremendous interest in fantasy among young people who read J. R. R. Tolkien's three-book series, *The Lord of the Rings*, sales of Dungeons & Dragons continued to escalate. By 1978, TSR Hobbies was a bustling place of business, with 18 full-time employees and sales of over $2 million.

EXPANDING THE TOEHOLD

Gygax wanted to expand upon the toehold that his product had gained in the game industry. He and Blume took a critical look at Dungeons & Dragons to see how it could be improved. They saw two possible problems. First, some players were having problems with the amount of time required to prepare a game. Second, some of the new players who were intrigued by Dungeons & Dragons needed to have their imaginations jump-started. To solve both of these problems, TSR created additional manuals—*The Dungeon Masters Guide*, *Players Handbook*, and *Monster Manual*—and even put together collections of ready-to-use dungeon settings.

One thing that was not a problem, despite the warnings of the experts, was the incredible detail. In fact, according to Gary Gygax, "much of that detail went in there because the players wanted it." Dungeons & Dragons players were not content with merely facing dragons; they wanted to know what species of dragon they were facing. Gygax provided a detailed categorization of dragons, with brass being the most dangerous. Some of the detail required intensive research. For example, Gygax studied herbalist journals extensively because he wanted to

J. R. R. Tolkien's *The Lord of the Rings* is a classic tale of good versus evil set in a medieval-type world populated with humans and an array of characters such as wizards, orcs, dwarfs, elves, and little people called hobbits. Dungeons & Dragons and many of the role-playing games that followed are based on the beings and myths from Tolkien's series of books. Renewed interest in the books, published in the mid-1950s, was created by the release in 2001 of the first part of a three-film version of *The Lord of the Rings*.

Human   Half-Orc   Half-Elf   Dwarf   Elf   Gnome   Halfling

One of the first things a Dungeons & Dragons player must decide is what race to choose for his or her character. This and other attributes and abilities are written on character record sheets.

use authentic herbs and spices as ingredients in the herbs and spices chart (for making potions).

Gygax also used the popularity of his medieval game to launch a diverse line of publications, including fantasy fiction books and a magazine called *The Dragon*. TSR offered something to appeal to all levels of fantasy game players. For the experts, the company began to sponsor a national convention for role-playing game enthusiasts. On the other end of the scale, it came out with a simple board game for those too young to grasp the intricacies of the Dungeons & Dragons adventure.

By 1979, the role-playing frenzy that TSR had started swept much of the continent. One business analyst was moved to declare that the "recent growth of interest in role-playing is not just a passing fad; it's the birth of a major popular art form." Because the game relied so heavily on imagination and had few parts, it was easy to copy and adapt, and dozens of role-playing products hit the market. *Forbes* magazine estimated that North Americans spent $23 million on role-playing games in 1980, with Dungeons & Dragons reeling in about one-third of that. Well into the 1980s, more people played Dungeons & Dragons than all other role-playing games combined. By 1985, the game had sold eight million copies and inspired a popular cartoon show.

DECLINE OF TSR

Keeping a steady hand on a company with an explosive growth rate is a challenging task for business experts, much less a do-it-yourself game inventor like Gygax. Yet, as president of TSR from 1976-1981, Gygax made sound financial decisions. Corporate long-term debt was low. Gygax borrowed money only for short-term needs that he quickly repaid. The company posted a profit of over $4 million on sales of $16.5 million in 1981.

But the role-playing game market was uncharted territory. It could change without warning and go off in unforeseen directions. Just as TSR was riding a wave of publicity over its phenomenal success, it came under heavy attack from critics. Upset by the game's use of evil monsters and magic, some religious groups labeled it part of the occult and tried to have it banned. The National Coalition on Television Violence tried to link the game to 29 suicides.

TSR's supporters rushed to its defense. The game was endorsed by the Association for Gifted and Creative Children, which found that players would often go on to read William Shakespeare and Isaac Asimov, as well as Tolkien. Director Steven Spielberg used the game to test children's role-playing abilities in casting the movie *E. T.: The Extra-Terrestrial*. Educational experts praised the amount of math, reading, and drama involved in a typical role-playing adventure. As one parent wrote in support of TSR, "The kids are learning instead of just being entertained." The criticism, however, led TSR Hobbies to eliminate references to demons and devils and to include a caution against players identifying too heavily with their characters.

In the end, however, it was the company's board of directors and Gygax's partners that led to the demise of TSR. Gygax lost control of the company's operations after the board decided to reorganize. The Blumes borrowed millions of dollars and didn't pay any attention to the quality of TSR's products. Although Gygax protested and managed to keep the company on its feet for a while, there wasn't much he could do without control of the company. In 1985, he sold his interest to Lorraine Williams, a member of the board of directors.

In 1997, Williams, with $30 million in debt and the prospect of bankruptcy looming, sold TSR to Seattle's Wizards of the Coast, which still produces the game although it, in turn, was bought by toy industry giant Hasbro in 1999. Gygax and a partner started from scratch, forming Hekaforge Productions and launching a new line of fantasy products under the title Lejendary Adventure.

LEGACY

The company Gary Gygax founded is relatively insignificant in the toy industry. At its height, TSR

An advertisement for the books about Gary Gygax's newest creation, Lejendary Adventure

never hired even a fraction of the number of employees other major game companies did, and it lasted but a short time as an independent company.

Nonetheless, Gygax's influence on the game industry is profound. In the words of *The Complete Book of War Games*, "Virtually single-handedly, Dungeons & Dragons established . . . what is essentially an entire new hobby." Gygax took a small segment of the game market—the war game—and totally reconstructed it into a noncompetitive exercise in creativity. The role-playing game that he pioneered turned out to fill a huge void—it provided an outlet for personality and imagination that other games did not provide.

The role-playing phenomenon that Gygax helped trigger has now grown into a billion-dollar-per-year industry. Magic: The Gathering, released by Wizards of the Coast in 1993, was the first of several wildly popular RPGs played with trading cards. Individual cards that were rare or powerful often sold for many times more than an entire "starter" pack of cards. Legend of the Five Rings was another successful Wizards card game; the company also printed Nintendo's Pokemon cards.

RPGs have spread into the video game and computer game markets. Technology has also allowed RPGs to reach the Internet, where thousands of players meet in cyberspace. Many computer games, such as Blizzard's Warcraft, come in both single-player and online versions. Other games, such as Everquest, are designed exclusively for Internet users, who pay a monthly fee to play.

Magic: The Gathering cards

An online version of Dungeons & Dragons made by BioWare in Edmonton, Alberta, Canada, was released in 2002. Neverwinter Nights allows players to create their own worlds, or be a Dungeon Master and control all the creatures and characters in a game that up to 64 people can log on and join. In its various forms, Dungeons & Dragons continues to hold its share of the RPG market and remains a favorite game of millions of hobbyists worldwide.

A view of how Neverwinter Nights looks on the computer screen to a player of the game

GLOSSARY

bankrupt: having been legally determined unable to pay back one's debts

bit: a single-digit number that represents zero or one in computer language and is the smallest unit of computer data, from the term "binary digit"

central processing unit: the part of the computer that carries out instructions

chip: a tiny electric circuit that may contain millions of electronic parts. Chips store instructions that run computers and process data.

contract: a legally binding, written agreement between two or more people

depression: a period of drastic decline in business production and of high unemployment

dry-cell battery: a battery that produces electricity using an outer case of zinc (negative pole) filled with a paste of chemicals and a carbon rod in the middle (positive pole)

gauge: the width between the outside rails of a train track

integrated circuit: an electronic circuit etched on a tiny chip of germanium or silicon that holds thousands of electronic elements

invest: to commit money to some enterprise, usually a business, in order to get more money or some other value in return

lease: a contract granting the use of property for a specified time in exchange for payment

lithography: a process in which an image is transferred to a sheet of metal, which is then treated to absorb ink in areas that will be printed and to repel ink in areas to be blank

merger: an agreement that combines two or more corporations into one

microprocessor: the complex chip that is the central processing unit of a computer

modem: a device that transmits data between two computers over telephone wires

revenue: income from an investment, business, or property

role-playing game (RPG): a game in which players act out or discuss scenarios in the role of characters they've chosen or had assigned to them

scale model: a small copy of an object made in proportion to the real object, using the same relationship throughout

shareholder: someone who owns a portion of a company, in the form of shares of stock

stock market: a place where stocks and bonds are actively traded

ties: the wooden beams laid across the bed of railroad tracks to support the rails

wet-cell battery: a setup that utilizes wire, lead plates, and jars of acid to generate low-voltage electricity

BIBLIOGRAPHY

"Albert Goodwill Spalding." http://www.spalding.com/history.html, cited February 7, 2002.

"Beware the Harpies." *Newsweek*, September 24, 1979.

Boritt, Gabor S., ed. *The Historian's Lincoln: Pseudohistory, Psychohistory, and History.* Urbana, Ill.: University of Illinois Press, 1988.

Carlson, Pierce. *Toy Trains: A History.* New York: Harper & Row, 1986.

Cleary, David Powers. *Great American Brands: The Success Formulas That Made Them Famous.* New York: Fairchild, 1981.

Coupland, Douglas. "Toys That Bind." *The New Republic*, June 30, 1994.

"The Creative World of Gary Gygax." http://www.gygax.com, cited February 7, 2002.

Cross, Gary. *Kids' Stuff: Toys and the Changing World of American Childhood.* Cambridge, Mass.: Harvard University Press, 1997.

Dickson, Paul. *The Mature Person's Guide to Kites, Yo-Yos, Frisbees and Other Childlike Diversions.* New York: New American Library, 1977.

Fine, Gary Alan. *Shared Fantasy: Role-Playing Games As Social Worlds.* Chicago: University of Chicago Press, 1983.

Freedman, Russell. *Lincoln: A Photobiography.* New York: Clarion, 1987.

Freeman, Jon, ed., with the editors of *Consumer Guide. The Complete Book of Wargames.* New York: Simon and Schuster, 1980.

Grabowski, John F. *Baseball.* San Diego: Lucent, 2001.

Gross, Neil. "No More Playing Around." *Business Week*, February 21, 1994.

Handler, Ruth, with Jacqueline Shannon. *Dream Doll: The Ruth Handler Story.* Stamford, Conn.: Longmeadow Press, 1994.

"History." http://www.lego.com/eng/info/history.asp, cited February 7, 2002.

Hollander, Ron. *All Aboard! The Story of Joshua Lionel Cowen and His Lionel Train Company.* New York: Workman, 1981.

"How Pong Invented Geekdom." *U.S. News & World Report*, December 17, 1999.

Jeffrey, Laura S. *Great American Businesswomen.* Springfield, N.J.: Enslow, 1996.

Johnson, Stancil. *Frisbee*. New York: Workman, 1975.

Levine, Peter. *A. G. Spalding and the Rise of Baseball: The Promise of American Sport*. New York: Oxford University Press, 1985.

"Lionel History." www.lionel.com/CentralStation/Findex.cfm

MacRae, Paul. "The Art of War for Fun and Profit." *MacLeans*, April 21, 1980.

"Mattel History." http://www.mattel.com/about_us/history/mattel_history.pdf, cited February 7, 2002.

Moskowitz, Milton, Robert Levering, and Michael Katz, eds. *Everybody's Business: A Field Guide to the 400 Leading Companies in America*. New York: Doubleday, 1990.

Pickering, David. *The Ultimate Lego Book*. New York: DK Publishing, 1999.

Pollack, Andrew. "Nintendo Chief Is All Work & No Play." *The New York Times*, August 26, 1996.

"Sega Company History." http://www.sega.com/segascream/legacy/history.jhtml, cited February 7, 2002.

Shea, James. *It's All in the Game*. New York: Putnam's Sons, 1960.

Sheff, David. *Game Over: How Nintendo Zapped an American Industry, Captured Your Dollars, and Enslaved Your Children*. New York: Random House, 1993.

———. "Mario's Big Brother." *Rolling Stone*, January 9, 1992.

Shenker, Israel. "Legoland, Where Business Is Child's Play." *Smithsonian*, June 1988.

Smith, Geoffrey. "Dungeons and Dollars." *Forbes*, September 15, 1980.

Souter, Gerry and Janet. *Lionel: America's Favorite Toy Trains*. Osceola, Wis.: MBI Publishing, 2000.

Vare, Ethlie Ann, and Greg Ptacek. *Women Inventors & Their Discoveries*. Minneapolis: The Oliver Press, 1993.

Werner, Rex. "From Bytes to Bites." *Variety*, June 26, 1995.

Whitehill, Bruce. *Games: American Boxed Games and Their Makers*. Radnor, Penn.: Wallace-Homestead, 1992.

Witchel, Alex. "A Spring in Her Step, James Has Been Making Slinkys 50 Years." *New York Times News Service*, reprinted in Minneapolis *Star Tribune*, February 25, 1996.

SOURCE NOTES

Quoted passages are noted by page and order of citation.

Introduction

p. 8 (first): Paul Dickson, *The Mature Person's Guide to Kites, Yo-Yos, Frisbees and Other Childlike Diversions* (New York: New American Library, 1977), 99.

p. 8 (second): Gary Alan Fine, *Shared Fantasy: Role-Playing Games As Social Worlds* (Chicago: University of Chicago Press, 1983), 5.

pp. 12-13: Gary Cross, *Kids' Stuff: Toys and the Changing World of American Childhood* (Cambridge, Mass.: Harvard University Press, 1997), 12.

p. 16 (first): Cross, *Kids' Stuff*, 4.

p. 16 (second): Cross, *Kids' Stuff*, 5.

p. 18: Stancil Johnson, *Frisbee* (New York: Workman, 1975), 19.

p. 21: Cross, *Kids' Stuff*, 196.

p. 23: Alex Witchel, "A Spring in Her Step, James Has Been Making Slinkys 50 Years," *New York Times News Service*, reprinted in Minneapolis *Star Tribune*, February 25, 1996, E9.

Chapter One

p. 28: Gabor S. Boritt, ed., *The Historian's Lincoln: Pseudohistory, Psychohistory, and History* (Urbana, Ill.: University of Illinois Press, 1988), 51.

p. 29: Russell Freedman, *Lincoln: A Photobiography* (New York: Clarion, 1987), 62.

p. 35: Bruce Whitehill, *Games: American Boxed Games and Their Makers* (Radnor, Penn.: Wallace-Homestead, 1992), 71.

Chapter Two

p. 46: David Powers Cleary, *Great American Brands: The Success Formulas That Made Them Famous* (New York: Fairchild, 1981), 281.

p. 49: John F. Grabowski, *Baseball* (San Diego: Lucent, 2001), 11.

p. 51: Cleary, *Great American Brands*, 282.

Chapter Three

p. 59: Ron Hollander, *All Aboard! The Story of Joshua Lionel Cowen and His Lionel Train Company* (New York: Workman, 1981), 191.

p. 60 (margin): Hollander, *All Aboard!*, 47.

p. 61: Hollander, *All Aboard!*, 23.

p. 62 (margin): Hollander, *All Aboard!*, 14.

p. 63 (caption): Hollander, *All Aboard!*, 27.

p. 64 (caption): Hollander, *All Aboard!*, 35.

p. 66: Hollander, *All Aboard!*, 44.

p. 67: Hollander, *All Aboard!*, 44.

p. 70 (first): Hollander, *All Aboard!*, 89.

p. 70 (second): Hollander, *All Aboard!*, 92.

p. 73 (caption): Hollander, *All Aboard!*, 50.

Chapter Four

p. 77: Ruth Handler with Jacqueline Shannon, *Dream Doll: The Ruth Handler Story* (Stamford, Conn.: Longmeadow Press, 1994), 58.

p. 79 (caption): Handler, *Dream Doll*, 67.

p. 79: Milton Moskowitz, Robert Levering, and Michael Katz, eds., *Everybody's Business: A Field Guide to the 400 Leading Companies in America* (New York: Doubleday, 1990), 276.

p. 80 (margin): Ethlie Ann Vare and Greg Ptacek, *Women Inventors & Their Discoveries* (Minneapolis: The Oliver Press, 1993), 7-8.

p. 83: Moskowitz, Levering, and Katz, *Everybody's Business*, 276.

p. 85: Vare and Ptacek, *Women Inventors*, 131.

Chapter Five

p. 92: Israel Shenker, "Legoland, Where Business Is Child's Play," *Smithsonian*, June 1988, 126.

p. 94: Shenker, "Legoland," 128.

p. 96: Shenker, "Legoland," 126.

p. 98: Cross, *Kids' Stuff*, 169.

p. 99: Cross, *Kids' Stuff*, 63.

p.101: Cross, *Kids' Stuff*, 169.

p. 105: Cross, *Kids' Stuff*, 220.

pp. 107-108: Douglas Coupland, "Toys That Bind," *The New Republic*, June 30, 1994, 9.

Chapter Six

p. 112: David Sheff, *Game Over: How Nintendo Zapped an American Industry, Captured Your Dollars, and Enslaved Your Children* (New York: Random House, 1993), 14.

p. 114: Sheff, *Game Over*, 23.

p. 116 (first): "How Pong Invented Geekdom," *U.S. News & World Report*, December 17, 1999, 67.

p. 116 (second): "How Pong Invented Geekdom," 67.

p. 116 (third): Rex Werner, "From Bytes to Bites," *Variety*, June 26, 1995, 6.

p. 116 (fourth): Werner, "From Bytes to Bites," 6.

p. 117: Sheff, *Game Over*, 28.

p. 126 (margin): Sheff, *Game Over*, 420.

p. 126: Neil Gross, "No More Playing Around," *Business Week*, February 21, 1994, 71.

Chapter Seven

p. 132: Paul MacRae, "The Art of War for Fun and Profit," *MacLeans*, April 21, 1980, 48.

p. 134: Fine, *Shared Fantasy*, 14.

p. 138 (margin): Geoffrey Smith, "Dungeons and Dollars," *Forbes*, September 15, 1980, 138.

pp. 138-139: MacRae, "The Art of War for Fun and Profit," 48.

p. 140: Fine, *Shared Fantasy*, 15.

p. 141: Smith, "Dungeons and Dollars," 138.

p. 143: Fine, *Shared Fantasy*, 15.

p. 146: Jon Freeman, ed., et al., *The Complete Book of Wargames* (New York: Simon and Schuster, 1980), 243.

INDEX

Spalding, J. Walter (brother), 46
Spalding's Official Baseball Guide, 48, 49
Spalding Sports Worldwide, 56
Spenco, 86
Spielberg, Steven, 144
standard-gauge tracks, 67, 68, 71
Super Mario Brothers, 121, 123, 128
Super Nintendo System, 126

Tactics, 133
Teddy bear, 81
television, 37; toys advertised on, 16-17, 78-80, 89
Tener, John, 48
tennis, 50
Teresa doll, 84
Tinker Toys, 15
Tolkien, J. R. R., 141, 144
Tolstoy, Leo, 8
Toni doll, 81
Tonka Toys, 20, 21
Toys R Us, Inc., 16
Toy Story, 23
trains, toy, 16, 59, 73, 99; Lionel, 16, 60, 63-66, 67, 68, 69, 70-72, 73, 76; manufactured in Germany, 66, 68-69; power sources of, 60, 65, 66, 67, 69
Transformers, 21
TSR (Tactical Studies Rules) Hobbies, Inc., 20, 140, 141, 142, 143, 144, 145-146
Twister, 36

Uke-A-Doodle, 79
Union Pacific, 71

video games, 111, 146; origins of, 114-115, 116; produced by Nintendo, 115, 117, 118-119, 120, 122, 123, 125, 129; tech-nology of, 115, 116, 117, 118, 122, 125-126, 127
Virtual Boy, 126

W. & S. B. Ives, 31, 68-69, 70
Warcraft, 146
war games, 132-134, 136, 140, 146
Wells, H. G., 133
Western Publishing Company, 85
Wham-O Company, 18
Williams, Lorraine, 144-145
Wizards of the Coast, 144-145, 146
Women's National Basketball Association, 52
Woods, Tiger, 57
World War I, 15, 69, 72, 73
World War II, 36, 71, 77, 94, 99, 112

The Yale-Harvard Game, 35
Yamauchi, Fusajiro (great-grandfather), 112, 113
Yamauchi, Hiroshi: early years of, 112; as head of Nintendo, 22, 111, 113-114, 115, 117-120, 121, 122, 123, 124, 125, 126, 128; retirement of, 126; Seattle Mariners purchased by, 125; video games developed by, 115, 117, 118, 119
Yamauchi, Katsuhito (son), 113
Yamauchi, Kimi (mother), 112, 113
Yamauchi, Sekiryo (grandfather), 112, 113
Yamauchi, Shikanojo (father), 112, 113
Yamauchi, Tei (grandmother), 112, 113
yo-yo, 11

Zelda, 121
Zemby, Zachary, 77, 78
Zoetrope, 32-33

ABOUT THE AUTHOR

Nathan Aaseng is an award-winning author of more than 100 fiction and nonfiction books for young readers. He writes on subjects ranging from science and technology to business, government, politics, and law. Aaseng's books for The Oliver Press include five titles in the **Business Builders** series and nine titles in the **Great Decisions** series. He lives with his wife, Linda, and their four children in Eau Claire, Wisconsin.

PHOTO CREDITS

AP/Wide World Photos: pp. 110, 115, 121, 128

BioWare: p. 147

Corbis: pp. 116, 119, 124

Gary Gygax: pp. 130, 139, 145

Elliot Handler and Mattel: pp. 74, 79, 82, 84 (both), 87, 88

Hasbro: pp. 21, 24, 27, 28, 30, 33 (both), 34 (both), 37, 39

Hulton/Archive: p. 14

Betty James: p. 23

LEGO Company: pp. 2, 22, 90, 93, 94, 95, 96, 97 (both), 98, 100, 101, 102, 104, 106 (top), 108, 109

Library of Congress: pp. 6, 10, 12, 48, 49, 51, 81

Lionel: pp. 58, 62, 63, 64, 65, 67, 68, 71, 73

Carlo E. and Lori Lynn Lomeli: p. 17

Mall of America: p. 106 (bottom)

National Portrait Gallery, London: p. 11

Sega: p. 127

Spalding Sports Worldwide, Inc.: pp. 40, 45, 50, 52, 53, 57 (both)

Theosophical University Press: p. 55

Wham-O, Inc.: p. 19 (©2001 Wham-O, Inc. All Rights Reserved. Frisbee® is a trademark of Wham-O, Inc.)

Wizards of the Coast: pp. 135, 137, 142 (both), 146